200 EVERYDAY LETTERS

200
EVERYDAY LETTERS
FOR
ALL OCCASIONS

JAMES HARVEY

GOODWILL PUBLISHING HOUSE®
B-3 RATTAN JYOTI, 18 RAJENDRA PLACE
NEW DELHI -110008 (INDIA)

Published by
GOODWILL PUBLISHING HOUSE®
B-3 Rattan Jyoti, 18 Rajendra Place
New Delhi-110008 (INDIA)
Tel. : 25750801, 25820556
Fax : 91-11-25764396
E-mail : goodwillpub@vsnl.net
website : www.goodwillpublishinghouse.com

Printed & Bound at : Batra Art Press, New Delhi

PREFACE

All of us have to write letters at some time or the other. You may need to add a covering letter with a job application; or have to request the Principal of your college for fee concession; or want to ask your bank manager for an overdraft; or wish to congratulate a friend on his success in an election; or have to convey your sweet thoughts to your beloved; or you may run a retail business and need to order supplies from a wholesaler; or you may wish to write to potential customers to try and persuade them to buy your goods or services—in short, in every field of life, the importance of letter writing cannot be ignored.

A letter, like other forms of writing, reflects your personality. Your personality and your business, office, or organisation will be judged, among other things, by the letters you write. And this book provides a basic grounding in letter-writing to help you produce effective, well -presented letters. The book begins by outlining points you should keep in mind while writing letters, the main layout styles and the standard parts of a typical letter. This is followed by sample letters for various occasons.

The two hundred letters given as examples in the book are grouped into three broad subject areas, viz. Business, Official and Personal. Each section has a number of letters to deal with various situations in life. Still, you are unlikely to find exactly the letter you need for your purpose in every case, but the examples will provide guidance as to the correct tone and style to adopt, and a framework on which to base a letter. Even in those cases where you find the letter of your choice, you need not imitate the letter to the word. Indeed, your letters should be an expression of you, so you will want to make some changes in order to inject some of your own personality into them. The letters given here as examples are, of course, all imaginary, as are the names and addresses used. While letters of almost all sorts have been included, I have ignored the letters of strictly 'legal' nature which may need to be cited in litigation. Here the exact wording is important, and if you have such a letter to write you would be well advised to seek professional advice.

JAMES HARVEY

CONTENTS

B. OFFICIAL LETTERS

C. PERSONAL LETTERS

The Mechanics of Letter Writing

INTRODUCTION

The fast pace of modernity has not been an unmixed blessing as a number of human activities which had been considered an art in the past have been reduced to the level of utility only. Letter writing is one such field. In the good old days when the pace of life was blisfully placid, people took a lot of pain over letter writing which was regarded by the leisured classes as well as men of letters, a literary accomplishment of no less distinction. The letters of writers like Dr. Samuel Johnson, Oliver Goldsmith, Horace Walpole, Willian Cowper, Jonathan Swift, John Keats and Lord Byron—to name a few stalwarts of this art—are known for, apart from depth of thought, their literary craftsmanship.

So great was the fascination for letter writing among the educated classes of those days, that it gave rise to a new literary genre, that is, epistolatory writing. Samuel Richardson's famous novel 'Pamela' and Smollett's 'Humphrey Clinker' may be cited as good examples. Apart from these, the letters written by some great men are still valued for their literary craftsmanship as well as they idea they convey. Some of these are : Oliver Goldsmith's Letter from a Citizen of the World, Burke's Letters on a Regicide Peace; Lord Chesterfield's Letters to his Son, White's Natural History of Selborne, Nehru's Letters from a Father to his Daughter, etc.

1

But the modernity—with its advanced means of communication like the telegraph and telephone, and in recent times, E-mail and internet—has sounded a death knell for letter writing as an art. Although letter writing, as one of the useful activities of modern life, still survives yet letter writing is now looked upon strictly from utilitarian point of view. Hence, there is an emphasis on communicating our ideas precisely and effectively. Given below are some useful hints which may guide you in the matter of writing letters in the modern times.

POINTS TO REMEMBER WHILE WRITING LETTERS

1. The aim of the letter

Despite the variety of topics on which letters are written, they all have at least one of three purposes : to convey information; to prompt action; or to maintain a satisfactory communication. The purpose for which the letter is written is likely to affect the tone and style of your letter. So it is important to keep your general, as well as more specific aim in mind.

2. The person to whom your letter is addressed

If you know about your correspondent, you can write a more effective letter. So, try to put yourself in you correspondent's shoes so that you may be able to judge how he or she is likely to react. This may suggest ways in which you can improve your letter.

3. Courtesy and honesty

These qualities are important in a letter not merely because they are the correct way to behave, but also because you are committing yourself to paper. If you write anything impolite, even if it is used unwittingly, you may make an enemy where you wanted to win a friend. If you are writing a letter of complaint, think very carefully before choosing your words. Try not to be abusive or impolite.

4. Clarity of thoughts and expression

It is very important to organise your thoughts and note down the main points before writing or replying to a letter. It is also important that, having decided what you want to say, you express yourself in a way the recipient of your letter will understand. Try to use short words and short sentences which convey the message simply and clearly. Long words and complex grammatical constructions are not only difficult to read but are often imprecise. if you do sometimes use long words, check their meaning and spelling in a dictionary. It is surprising how often they do not convey quite the meaning you intended.

Do not try to use too much technical jargon, and avoid 'foreign' phrases where there is a simple and precise English equivalent. Your aim is to make your meaning clear to the recipient, and not to impress him with your knowledge.

5. Clinches and worn out phrases

Always avoid phrases such as 'We beg to acknowledge receipt of your letter' or 'Permit me to state' or 'I hope this letter will find you in the best of health and spirits'. Just go ahead and state an idea as if you were talking face to face with the recipient. It is better to write 'Thank you for your letter' instead of saying 'we beg to acknowledge the receipt of you letter.'

6. Accuracy and completeness

Your letter should always be dated. Check that the recipient's name and address are given correctly and spelt accurately. Read the letter again before putting it into the envelope. Check spelling, punctuation and grammer, any facts and figures and, finally, make sure you put the letter in the correct envelops.

LAYOUT AND STYLE

Although there is no one correct way to lay out a letter, it is important to develop an attractive and consistent style. The two major styles of letter layout are known as blocked (or fully blocked) and semi-blocked (also referred to as indented). Similarly, there are two punctuation styles : open and close punctuation.

The fully blocked and semi blocked (or indented) styles

These styles differ mainly in whether or not the paragraphs are indented, in the position of the date, any subject heading, and the complimentary close. The fully blocked style tends to give a more 'modern' look to a letter, but both styles are equally correct. The blocked style is usually used in business correspondence. However, you must maintain uniformity : these two styles should not be mixed within a letter.

The indented style differs from the blocked in having the recepient's address, the first line of each paragraph stepped, *i.e.* a few spaces away from the left alignment of the text. The complimentary close in such a style is shifted to the right and is aligned with the right side of the text. It is more appropriate for personal than for business or official correspondence. In this book, the blocked style has been used throughout.

Punctuation Styles—Open and Close Punctuation

The other main choice in style concerns the use of punctuation, which can be used in two ways. Open punctuation involves minimal punctuation and this method is normally used with the blocked style. In closed or full punctuation—which is also the traditional style— commas are used after the address lines and after the opening greeting and complimentary close.

Following two pages show examples of both the above styles.

Example 1. Fully blocked and open punctuation styles

DYANORA STEEL MILLS LTD.

345 Thana Road
Ankola
Tel. : 234876
Fax : 459875

October 26, ...

The General Manager
Asbestos Dickson Road,
13, Singapore.

Dear Sir,

We have been a customer of your company for a long time. Needless to say we have both benefited greatly from these mutual business relations. As a customer of long standing, we make a special request. At present we are passing through a lean patch. In cutting corners, we must limit expenditures that probably include our future purchases.

Keeping this in view, this company requests you to give us a further discount of 5% on our future purchases.

We thank you in advance for your consideration.

Hoping to get an early reply,

Sincerely yours,

General Manager

Example 2. Indented and closed punctuation style

SOUTHAMPTON ENTERPRISES

152, Bernard Avenue,
23, Southall Road,
London.
e-mail : se@britnet.in

September 26, ...

To

Mr. J. Clive
Queensland Marketing
45, Victoria Street
Gloucester (UK)

Dear Mr. Clive,

You will recall that this company placed an order for three superior yarn knitting machines which have not been received. We had made a special request for the early shipment of this item. You had promised to deliver the machines within the time agreed upon mutually. But dead line passed two weeks ago and still there is no sign of the consignment. We feel that this situation is not consistent with your customer satisfaction commitments.

Kindly let us know the status of our order immediately. Thank you for your assistance and prompt reply. Let me remind you once again that we are in urgent need of the yarn knitting machines for our new cloth mill.

Sincerely yours,

George Berkeley
General Manager

THE BASIC FRAMEWORK OF A LETTER

Although letters deal with a wide range of topics, it is possible to categorise the main parts of a typical letter. Most letters would not contain all these all these features, but they should all contain the essential parts, namely : the sender's address, date, the recipient's name and address, the opening salutation, message or the main body of the letter, a complimentary close, a signature and a sender's name.

(a) The sender's name and address

In both the blocked and indented styles the sender's name and address is usually typed at the top right of a letter, aligned on the longest line. The full postal address (including the country if the recipient knows exactly where to reply. In most of the business letters, the names and addresses are already included as part of the printed letter-heads.

(b) Reference code

Reference codes are generally used in business letters to help in filing or locating as also in replying letters. The reference code is usually given at the top left above the recepient's address or sometimes in the centre of the letter after the recepient's address.

(c) Date

The date should always be given in full and not in the form of numbers such a 5.3.19....... This can cause difficulty in international correspondence because in Britain the day is given first whereas in the United States the month is usually given first. Therefore 5.3.19...... could be read as 5th March 3rd May ! It is also much clearer no to abbreviate month names or years, and the year should always be included as it may be important in referring back to past correspondence for both you and the recipient.

(d) Recipient's name

If possible you should include the name of an individual recipient and at least a specific job title if it is a business or official letter. This makes the letter someone's particular responsibility and it may lead to a quicker reply. It may also be useful if you need to follow up the letter and want to know to whom you wrote in the past.

Courtesy titles. "An individual's name" should always be preceded by a courtesy title, and the spellings of names should be carefully written. The most common courtesy titles are 'Mr', 'Mrs.', 'Miss', or 'Ms' You may 'Esq.', (which indicated the status of 'gentleman' in the past), instead of Mr but it follows the name as, J Brown, Esq.). However, 'Mr' is probably the best courtesy title to use for most male recipients.

If a woman has indicated on past correspondence her preferred courtesy title you should use this. If not, and you are unsure as to her marital status, it is generally acceptable to use either 'Ms' or 'Miss'

Some courtesy titles are related to qualifications, professions or honours and replace the normal courtesy titles. These are : 'Prof.', 'Dr.', 'Rev.', 'Choudhary', 'Sir', etc. 'Dr.' or 'Doctor' can be used for a man or a woman, and is used if the person has a doctoral degree as well as for medical doctor's.

Sometimes letters denoting honours, qualifications or professions may be used after the name. But they should not be included unless these are particularly relevant. You may add MBBS to a doctor's name when writing to him in his professional capacity, but it would not sound proper to add 'M.A.' to a shop keeper's name just because you know he had a degree.

(e) Recipient's address

This should be copied carefully from the previous correspondence if available and should be the same as the address to be used on the envelope. The addresses generally include some or all of the following :

1. A building or house number (and a flat, chamber or office number if appropriate). No comma is needed after the number before the road name.
2. A road name
3. The name of the street
4. The name of the locality
5. A village name, or a district of a town if there are several streets of the same name in a town.

6. The postal town. This is the town where letters are sorted for local delivery.

7. The pin code.

8. Name of the country, if you are sending the letter abroad.

(f) Opening salutation (or greeting)

The opening salutation is used according to the way the recipient's name has been given.

If the letter is addressed to an individual the salutation would normally be in the form 'Dear Mr. Chaudhary', 'Dear Miss Dixit' etc., (*i.e* . the courtesy title and surname, but no initials or first names). If the recipient is a good and intimate friend, it would be appropriate to use the first name as, 'Dear John'. If the person has been addressed by office rather than by name, the greeting should be 'Dear Sir' or 'Dear Madam'.

If a whole department or business organisation is being addressed the salutation would be 'Dear sirs'.

(g) Subject heading

It is generally used in business and official correspondence. It is often helpful to both the sender and the recipient to give a subject heading immediately after the opening greeting. It should be short and concise and should match that given by your correspondent if you are continuing discussion of the same topic.

(h) Message, or the main body of a letter

Sometimes it is difficult to think of suitable words with which to start the letter. Given below are some of the openings. But the list is by no means exhaustive and you may use any opening that suits you.

With reference to your letter of ....

Thank you for your letter of ....

In reply to your letter of ....

I am delighted/glad/pleased to tell/inform you that ....

I regret/ am sorry to tell/inform you ....

9

I wish to draw your attention to ....

As requested ....

I am writing to ....

We recently wrote to you about ....

You may be interested to hear ....

We wish to remind you that ....

Referring to your letter of ....

I wonder if you could ....

I wish to ....

I enclose ....

Please ....

I am sorry to inform you that ....

We would like to know ....

I have to point out ....

We have carefully considered ....

Always refer to any previous correspondence in the first paragraph and also try to get to the point of the letter reasonably quickly without beating about the bush. It is best to start a paragraph with a 'topic sentence', that is, introducing the subject of the paragraph, as this will help your reader to follow your train of thought.

Avoid using a 'PS' in a letter. If your letter has been well planned last-minute thoughts and additions should be unnecessary.

(i) Complimentary close

This should match the opening greeting. Yours sincerely' or 'Yours faithfully' will be appropriate in nearly all cases. 'Your sincerely' is used where the individual is named, and 'Yours faithfully' where the salutation is 'Sir', 'Dear Sir' or similar.

Other complimentary closes include : 'Faithfully yours' or 'Sincerely yours' (which tend to sound a bit pompous), 'Yours respectfully', (sometimes for higher or closer and respectable persons), and 'Yours truly' (which can be used for friends, but it sounds a bit formal). 'Best wishes' or some other greeting would be more

10

appropriate if you know the recipient intimately and have addressed him as 'Dear John' or something similar.

(j) Signature

Letters will usually bear the signature of the writer; however, sometimes other conventions are followed. A partner signing for his firm, for example, should use the firm's name without adding his own name. In business letters it is considered discourteous to a firm's rubber stamp in place of a signature.

(k) Sender's name

Unless you are confident that your signature is readable, or it will be very familiar to your correspondent, it is as well to include your name immediately below the signature and this should match the signature.

ADDRESSING ENVELOPES

The envelope conveys the first impression of your letter so it is important that the address on it should be legibly written or neatly typed. The wording of the address should be as given in the letter. The address should start about halfway down the envelope, leaving at least 40 mm (1.5 inches) or so above for the stamp and the postal mark.

All the parts of the address should have separate lines as this make it easier for the postal services to deal with the letter quickly and efficiently. The PIN (postal index number) code should always be at the end of the address. Any classification such as 'PERSONAL', 'CONFIDENTIAL', etc. should be indicated on the envelope (a couple of lines above the name and address). If the letter is sent through the postal service other than normal, such as 'Registered.' 'By Air mail', 'Through courier,' 'Speed post', 'under postal certificate,' etc. write these words at the top centre of the envelope.

The sender's name and address is generally written in the left bottom corner, but some business house prefer to put in the top left corner.

Business
Letters

I. PLACING AND CANCELLATION OF ORDERS; SUPPLIES AND EXECUTION

1. Letter for placing an order [from a firm to another firm]

AHMED AND SONS

25 Jalan Sultan
Kuala Lumpur
Phone : 2357986, 2357988
Fax : 2357977
E-mail : dds@dds. renet.

September 25, ...

The Manager (Supplies)
Pravez Tubes and Pipes Pvt Ltd
14, Leboh China
Penang

Dear Sir

Kindly refer to your quotations for the supply of steel pipes and pvc pipes which we require in connection with the construction of our new plant at Badodar.

We are pleased to inform you that your quotations for these and allied items have been approved. You are, therefore, requested to supply us the following items within one month, FOR Kuala Lumpur as stipulated in your terms and conditions of your offer.

1. Steel pipes, half inch   3000 nos.

2. PVC pipes for water fittings   2250 nos.

3. PVC sprinklers with fittings for lawns   450 nos.

4. Plastic water storage tanks capacity 50 litres   90 nos.

We expect that professional attention will be given to our order for the above items.

As agreed to between us in our telephonic talk, we need credit for three months for making payment for the above items. Thereafter we will pay you interest at the rate of 18% for the time we take in making payment.

I look forward to a long, professional relationship between our two firms.

Sincerely yours

V. Jackson
General Manager

Kenny Chan
354, Nathan Road
Kowloon

August 3, ...

M/s Goodwill Publishing House
Paya Thai Road
Bangalore

Dear Sirs

I am in need of the following books for my personal use. You are requested to kindly send them at an early date :

1. Sports Quiz Book by M.R. Sethi   2 copies

2. Science Quiz by M.R. Sethi   1 copy

3. 250 Challenging Puzzles   2 copies

4. Top Winning letters   1 copy

Kindly send the books by registered post together with your bill. I shall remit the amount by bank draft immediately on receipt of the packet.

Please ensure that the books are in good condition and are packed properly.

Thank you

Yours faithfully

Kenny Chan

GEM GENERAL HOSPITAL

234, Rizal Avenue,
Manila
Tel : 5436654
Fax : 632-5437765

September 25, ...

M/s Globe Surgical Industries
457, Sector 18-B
Shanghai

Dear Sirs

Kindly refer to our order placed vide our letter no. 765/98 dated 10th September. The order was placed on the basis of information available at the time.

Unfortunately, new information makes it necessary for us to cancel the order immediately. The details surrounding cancellation are confidential. I have personally checked your cancellation policies and confirmed that we are in compliance with them.

Believe me, if I were at liberty to provide a full explanation, I would. However, I hope that this cancellation would not affect our cordial business relations.

Thanking you

Yours faithfully

Administrative Officer (Stores)

LARSEN AND TOUBRO

8, Musuem Street
London
E-mail : @gems.vsnl.net.in
September 19, ...

Mr. Morris Brandet
General Manager
Sylavania and Laxman Electric Co.
Derby.

Dear Mr. Brandet

Kindly refer to our order dated August 25 ...... regarding the supply of electrical equipment for our factory at Georgetown. I wish to point out that the supplies have not reched us so far although in my telephonic conversation with you on the first of this month I had apprised you of our immediate need for the said items.

Under normal conditions, I would not ask for special arrangements for delivery of goods. But as circumstances are beyond my control, I would request you that the goods should be in our possession not later than the end of this month.

Before shipment, please obtain my approval on any additional charges required by you to accommodate our request. I look forward to receiving confirmation that our request is being handled. Your professional assistance in ensuring delivery within these time limitations is greatly appreciated.

With warm regards

Sincerely yours

Cooper C
General Manager

REXONA PAINTS AND HARDWARE SUPPLIERS

375, East of Jama Masjid
Jakarta
Tel : 5678765
Fax : 5678993

August 16, ...

M/s Asian Paints
765, Jln. Ibrahim
Bali

Dear Sirs

Please send us a catalogue of your full range of paints, wood and metal primers and distempers. Please also supply us with details regarding trade terms such as discounts, incentives, credit, shipment, guarantee on products, the period allowed for making payment, etc.

At the same time, kindly let us know how soon we might expect delivery after placing an order and what the position is regarding your after-sales service.

Thanking you

Yours faithfully

for Sam P&H Store

General Manager

KIRLOSKAR FERROUS PRIVATE LTD

345, B.D. Road
Chungmai
Tel. 234876
Fax : 459875

September 26, ...

Mr. Ashok Mittal
General Manager
Asbestos India Ltd.
323, M.G. Road
Phuket

Dear Mr. Mittal

We have been a dedicated customer of your company for a long time. Needless to say we have both benefited greatly form these mutual business relations. As a customer of long standing, we have a special request to make. The current economy forces us to become lean and mean in our competitive stance. In cutting corners, we must limit expenditures that probably include our future purchases.

Based on our relationship, it is my hope that you will help us with our cost-saving measures. This company requests that we be given a further discount of 5% on our future purchases.

We thank you in advance for your consideration.

Hoping to get an early reply,

Sincerely yours

R. Somkhun
General Manager

BERKELEY ENTERPRISES

25 Oakley Avenue
23, Northants
London
E-mail : BE@britnet.in

September 26, ...

Mr. J. George
Kingley Marketing
64 King Street
Manchester (UK)

Dear Mr. George

In today's business, our lives are becoming increasingly globally oriented. The advanced technology and means of transportation have made it possible for goods as well as people to move at speeds much higher than in the past. It's routine to expect a package from Los Angeles to arrive at its London destination in no more than 48 hours.

However, I am concerned that we placed an order for three superior yarn knitting machines which have not been received. We had made a special request for the early shipment of this item. Your company had promised timely delivery. We feel that this situation is not consistent with your customer satisfaction commitments.

I call it to your attention to advise me on the status of our order immediately. Thank you for your assistance and prompt replay. Let me remind you once again that we are in urgent need of the yarn knitting machines for our new cloth mill.

Sincerely yours

George Berkeley
General Manager

ZULFI AND SONS LTD.

345 Lawrence Road
Lahore
Fax. 4348837
E-mail : SRS@elec.01.vsnl.in

October 23, ...

The General Manager
Khyam Telecom Ltd
654 Circular Road
Karachi

Today, customer satisfaction and operational goals are intertwined in companies of high ethical standing. So what you buy is not as important as who you buy from. It was this in view that we bought electronic equipment worth 10 lakhs from you.

We are, however, sorry to point out that one of the items purchased from you has disappointed us. Based on your company's claims of 100 percent satisfaction through a money-back guarantee, we willingly purchased high fidelity dish antennas, along with other items form you. But these antennas do not meet our performance or quality expectations. We are returning these antennas through road transport.

We have already spent much time and effort acquiring this item. It is our hope that no more of either will be required to receive our rightful 100 percent refund of the purchase price.

We do hope to have your prompt attention.

Sincerely yours

Z. Zulfi
Managing Director

MARK TAYLOR AND COMPANY LTD.

549, Evergreen Street
Calcutta
Tel : 2764389, 2768731
Fax : 09133-2767377
E-mail : SWC@intnet.in

July 13, ……

The Managing Director
Shaw Wallace and Company
New Delhi 110001

Dear Sir

This has a reference to your letter dated ninth August, requesting us to quote our rates for a few items of your interest. This request has presented us with a unique challenge. I have spent much time formulating a time-based action plan to be used in completing the bid for the requisite items. Resources have been distributed with the obvious goal of winning your business.

This company has a reputation for delivering superb bid responses to its customers. I fear that submitting anything less may jeopardize our professional standing. In order for us to uphold this standard, we request an extension of the due date from these items.

The extra time will permit us to deliver a document worthy of your business and praise. If possible, please confirm this extension through fax or E-mail at your earliest convenience.

Thank you for your professional courtesy in this matter. I consider a bid response more than a document; it is a direct reflection of our commitment to customer satisfaction.

Sincerely yours

General Manager

FLEX LTD.

487-K/2, Byron Road
Colombo
Tel : 437982, 437986
Fax : 0941-437788

August 25, ...

The General Manager
Westworth Enterprises Ltd.
Kandy

Dear Sir

We are thankful to you for your letter dated 10th August, asking us to bid for certain items concerning heavy electrical machinery. You will agree that preserving a reputation for excellence is demanding. After going through the specifications of the machinery demanded by you, we were faced with a difficult decision. Of course, we want to have business links with a reputed company like yours, yet we are not sure that we can adhere to our usual high quality standards.

It is always painful to turn down potential business. Unfortunately, however, this letter is a formal notification that we are not responding to the aforementioned bid. Please do not interpret this as a lack of desire to establish a long-term business relationship with your company.

We hope that other opportunities more in line with our areas of expertise and specialization will materialize. Then, we'll have the chance to demonstrate our unparalleled dedication and professionalism. I look forward to those opportunities.

With best regards,

Sincerely yours

Works Manager

II. ADJUSTMENTS/COMPLAINTS ABOUT BILLING

11. Accountant's bill

BILL GATES COMPUTERS

76, North street
Broadford Avenue
Washington, D.C.
Tel. : 986543
E-mail : GGC@wash.net.in

July 25, ...

M/s Cassius Clay and Sons
Chartered Accountants
54, North East Trade Centre
Washington, D.C.

Dear Sirs

By now, you've probably noticed that Bill Gates Computers is a bottom-line-oriented company constantly checking and double-checking its facts and figures. Although your firm has done a fine job managing our books and advising us on tax matters, I question the calculations on the latest bill we received. The total amount due is not reasonable, and I'm sure a review will result in a favourable adjustment Bill Gates Computers.

We appreciate our affiliation with you, but I cannot justify bills of this nature. You have always handled our statements very professionally, so I ask that you personally analyze this bill and the amount owed to us.

Thank you in advance for your assistance.

Sincerely yours

Apple Mackintosh
General Manager

RAKAL AND KAJAL LTD.

98/P, Parkison Road
Singapore
June 10, ...

M/s Ross Murarka & Sons
432 Jln. Bulia
Ipoh

Dear Sirs

In today's computer age, information management is generally thought to be absolutely faultless. But there is no doubt that mistakes still happen. We can understand that just one incorrect keystroke can add the wrong column of figures or erase an entire file of customer requests. It appears that this was the case on invoice number 005796 recently sent by you.

Upon checking our records regarding the purchase of tinned food items, we have discovered that bill contains an error. The correct amount should be $ 45, 975 and not $ 75, 975. I am confident that your firm's due diligence will result in the correction of the bill.

We appreciate that computers are merely machines and only as good as the humans who control them. We are prone to error, and so are the machines.

Thank you in advance for your prompt attention in this matter.

With best regards,
Sincerely yours

General Manager

SHEENA PVT. LTD.

56/A S.P.M. Road
Brunei
Tel : 5465537

June 19, ...

Mr. Rashid
Managing Director
Datta Lawyers Pvt. Ltd.
45, Shafiq Palace
Brunei

Dear Mr. Rashid

We are fortunate to have business relations with a reputed firm of lawyers such as yours. Needless to say we have benefited greatly from your professional experience and dedication to the satisfaction of your clients.

I am, however, sorry to point out that I was shocked when I received your recent bill for your services regarding handling our case for violation of FERA. The bill is quite exaggerated and much more than our expectations. Perhaps we have simply had a misunderstanding over fees and expenses. It is also possible that my records have somehow been confused with those of another client.

Therefore, I ask you to review the bill in the light of the terms agreed upon between us before you took up our case and advise me of your position as soon as possible.

I thank you for professional courtesy in this matter.

With best regards,

Sincerely yours

Sheena
Managing Director

THOMPSON PRESS

432, Main Market
Dhaka
E-mail. TP@vsnl.in.net
Tel. : 2937165, 2937175

August 16, ...

M/s Dhaka Paper Mills
7-B, Munger Chowk
Chitgong

Dear Sirs

This has a reference to your bill no. 5439 dated 1st August. We were shocked to receive the bill as the items mentioned in the bill have not been ordered by us.

The bill concerns newsprint and the art paper for covers of magazines. On the other hand we had placed an order for ledger quality paper for printing of high quality books which we have already received. It is clear that there has been an inadvertent mistake in your billing section and the bill meant for some other firm has been sent to us.

We can appreciate that sometimes mistakes do happen. You are requested kindly to send us a revised bill for the things supplied to us so that we may make the payment at an early date.

Thanking you

Yours sincerely

Managing Director

CLASSIC COMPUTERS

987, The Shopping Mall
Jalan Sultan
Kuala Lumpur

November 30, ...

Mr. Dilshad
Sales Manager
M/s Hewett Packard Ltd
Jalan Ramla
Sabah

Dear Mr. Dilshad

Ours is a consumer-conscious company. So we follow standard buying etiquette. Purchases are investigated and opinions gathered before our company authorizes spending.

Our experience with computer peripherals bought on the 10th of this month for $ 5655, does not match the product literature or testimonial claims. Specifically. The computer printing cartridges and floppies prove to be below standard level in the following manner :

(*a*) The computer cartridges for dot matrix printers have come shabbily packed. A few items were found damaged.

(*b*) The ink cartridges for desk jet printers are not of the expected quality.

(*c*) A few floppies were tested at random and we are sorry to inform you that about 15 per cent of them were found to be defective.

We are returning the defective/substandard material through the couriers. It is my hope that a refund including the cost incurred by us in sending the material back will be expedited to protect our opinion of your company.

We have always believed that any product should, at the very minimum, leave a buyer satisfied with his or her purchase and the company that sold it.

We look forward to the immediate refund that will help us to continue maintaining good business relations with you.

Sincerely yours

P. Swindon
for Classic Computers

VICHAI BUILDERS PVT. LTD.

65 Vichai Shopping Complex
Wang Burapha, Bangkok
E-mail : ABPL@mod.net.in.
Tel. : 2379813, 2378557

July 29, ...

M/s Otis Elevators
453 D.K. Road
Chungmai

Dear Sirs.

We have maintained good business relations with your firm over the last many years. Unfortunately now it seems that unless something is done urgently from your side, our relations are under the threat of cooling off.

I hope you understand that I am referring to the work undertaken by you to provide escalators and lifts in the Hotel Madonna which has been constructed by our firm.

When our engineers checked the elevator in the rear block of the hotel, they found that it was not functioning properly. It jammed on more than one occasion. This was pointed out to the Works Engineer of your company as early as fifteen days ago, but inspite of his assurance to rectify the fault soon, he has done nothing in this matter. I am sorry to point out that this is a very serious matter as the hotel is to be inaugurated in a month's time from hence and the reputation of our construction firm is at stake.

Let me point out that if the fault in the elevator is not rectified within a week, we will not only be constrained to get it repaired from another firm but also to deduct the charges from your bill. At the same time, it will cast a shadow on our business relations.

You are aware that bad news spreads like wildfire. Your shoddy handling of our business is very likely to tarnish your image in the business world. However, I hope that you will not let it happen by taking a prompt action in the matter.

Sincerely yours

M.N. Keree
Managing Director

THOMPSON GENERAL SUPPLIERS

341, Thompson Street
Main Bazar
Kandy

March July 20, ...

M/s Preeti Latex Works
14, Galle Road
Colombo

Dear Sirs

We have had very good business relations for about a decade now. During this period we have given you a lot of business. Therefore, we expect that when a firm of our standing makes an inquiry concerning a product, it must be attended to on priority basis. However, I am sorry to point that this does seem to have been so in the recent few months.

I have contacted your company on several occasions during the last one month regarding supply of specially made raincoats, but no response has been received from you so far. I know that this is a little unconventional item. But as a professional I believe that this is not an insurmountable dilemma you have made up your mind to help a customer of long standing.

Let me point out that your unprofessionalism is destroying any possibility of future business with us. I hope to hear from you within the next week.

With regards

Sincerely yours

D. Thompson
General Manager

GLORY FANS PVT LTD

457, Karunanidhi Marg
Egmore

June 12, ...

The General Manager
Alva Electric Company
345, T. Nagar
Chennai

Dear Sir

This has a reference to you notification dated 8th June. Let me tell you that this letter has disappointed us. Pardon my anger over receiving notification that Alva Electric co. has increased the price dramatically for condensers for ceiling fans.

I find it inconceivable that you have taken this ludicrous step inspite of the stiff competition in the market for this item. You are forcing many established customers, like Glory Fans to look elsewhere for their supplies. You are not the only company selling condensers for fans. I am sorry to point out that the solid relationships between seems to be ending.

This is precisely why I have chosen to express my disappointment through this letter. Up to now, your professional practices were quite respectable and consistent with our own. As this is no longer the case, I want to tell you that we are evaluating other sources for our needs.

I hope you will not like to let some other company to edge you out of the favour of so solid as a company as ours. If this is possible, please telephone at your earliest convenience. I hope to hear from you shortly.

Sincerely yours

Mohan Rakesh
Procurement Manager

GEORGE INDUSTRIES LIMITED
[Steel Furniture Division]

5, World Trade Centre
Singapore

October 21, ...

M/s Jeena Furniture Suppliers
346, Tiang Road
Seoul

Dear Sirs

The customer's satisfaction is our primary concern. Thank you for informing us of a possible discrepancy regarding our bill for plastic moulded furniture which we supplied to you last month. We encourage customers to contact us when such situations arise.

However, after extensively going through the records of our transactions with you, we have found that no mistakes were made and the bill is correct as stated. The rates mentioned in the bill are exactly those stated by us in our quotations and the items supplied have been strictly as per your order.

If you require any additional information about the transaction, by all means, call or write again. We are always here when you need us, and we thank you for your past and future business.

Sincerely yours

Samanta
General Manager

GEORGE INDUSTRIES LIMITED
[Steel Furniture Division]

5, World Trade Centre
Worli, Singapore

October 21, ...

M/s Jeena Furniture Suppliers
346, Tiang Road
Seoul

Dear Sirs

Thank you for your letter dated 10th October, apprising us of an error in our bill for plastic moulded furniture supplied to you last month. We have checked our records and found that your complaint is genuine. Let us assure you that no defense exists for a situation that jeopardizes customer satisfaction. We value your association with us more than anything else.

We have made an immediate change in the bill and the new bill reflects strictly the rates which had been quoted by us in our bid. The items which had been left out inadvertently but had been charged for in the bill are being despatched to you post haste. In the mean time we are making arrangements to get back, at our cost, the items wrongly supplied to you.

Thank you for bringing this matter to our attention. This company always considers it beneficial when customers feel comfortable pointing out areas in which we fall below our high standards.

Sincerely yours

Samanta
General Manager

III. LETTERS REGARDING PAYMENT

21. Casual reminder for payment

FOUR SQUARES LIMITED
(Sports Goods Division)

54-A, Mandaloyong
Manila
E-mail. FSI@vsnl.int.in

January 12, ...

M/s Steve Sports Dealers
659, Safidon Road
Saigon

Dear Sirs

Modern life has become so hectic that sometimes we forget to do even simple things like reading the newspaper. I believe that it is because of your busy schedule that you have forgotten to make payment for our bill No. 432 dated 13th November for the sports goods supplied to you.

We have always maintained good relations with your firm. Your credit history suggests that simple neglect is the reason for your lack of promptness in remitting our payment. Our records indicate that the amount of $ 12,125 is due to you.

We request you kindly to make payment of the bill at an early date. If you have already despatched the cheque by the time this letter reaches you, please accept my apologies for this friendly reminder.

Thank you for your assistance.

Sincerely yours

Lin U Tang
Manager

FOUR SQUARES LIMITED
(Sports Goods Division)

54-A, Chowranghee Square
Frankfurt
E-mail.FSI@vsnl.int.in
Tel. : 8765412
Fax : 8787871

January 12, ...

Mr. Stevenson
General Manager
M/s Gem Sports Dealers
659, Safidon Road
Munich

Dear Mr. Stevenson

In the modern business world both the suppliers and customers have obligations. Suppliers provide high-quality goods and services; customers, in returns, pay for those goods and services on the agreed upon terms. Sometimes, companies take payment matters lightly, failing to consider that suppliers must carry the burden for late-paying customers.

The Four Squares has lived up to our side of the bargain; you have fallen behind. Because of the credit rating of your company, we extended ourselves to the point of providing references when you applied for credit with other companies.

By sending payment for our bill dated 13th November immediately, you will make your account current and protect your credit rating. God credit ratings take years to establish and only months to destroy. Kindly send the payment of the bill by the end of this month. If there are any extenuating circumstances which prevent you from complying with our request for payment, please call me today.

Thank you for your prompt attention.

Sincerely yours

Peter
Manager

FOUR SQUARES LIMITED
(Sports Goods Division)

54-A, Chowranghee Square
Frankfurt
E-mail.FSI@vsnl.int.in
Tel. : 8765412
Fax : 8787871

January 12, ...

The General Manager
M/s Gem Sports Dealers
659, Safidon Road
Munich

Dear Sir

Kindly refer to our bill No. 243 dated 12th August for the supply of sports goods to you. Thereafter a number of letters reminding you to expedite the payment have not borne fruit. In every management meeting, we discuss with disbelief the fact that your company continues to shirk its obligations. The outstanding balance of $ 45,500 overdue by months.

I am responsible for our company's accounting, and your lack of action has forced me to cancel all future extensions of credit. Our company has always maintained good relations with you and it is because of these relations that we have decided to offer you two options that will allow you to fulfill your obligations :

1. Remit the full amount of $ 45,500; or
2. Remit a partial payment of Rs. 25,000 with the undertaking that the balance is to be paid within the next two months.

We would like our mutual good relations to continue. However, only a positive response from you can allow this to happen.

With kind regards,

Sincerely yours

Peter

FOUR SQUARES LIMITED
(Sports Goods Division)

54-A, Chowranghee Square
Frankfurt
E-mail : FSI@vsnl.int.in

January 12, ...

The General Manager
M/s Gem Sports Dealers
659, Safidon Road
Munich

Dear Sir

Kindly refer to our bill No. 243 dated 12th June, ... for the supply of sports goods to you. Our file is thick with reminders sent to you requesting an early payment to our bill. Gem Sports Goods Dealers have always been a valued customer of ours, and we are confused by the change in your payment history.

An amount of $ 35,700 is overdue and I once again request you to make the payment of this amount at an early date.

If the payment is not made within a month, we will be constrained to take the matter to the court. To date, I have personally gone out of my way to see that such action is not taken with your company because we have had good business relations for a number of years.

If there is some problem with you and we can be of help, let us discuss the issue before I am forced to take recourse to law. Your promptness in settling the matter can still salvage our mutual relations.

With regards,

Sincerely yours

Peter
Manager

TIRUPATI STARCH LIMITED

321, Egmore Road
Vellore. (TN)

October 22, ...

M/s Raman Chemicals Pvt. Ltd.
658, North Avenue
Banglore

Dear Sirs

I wish to draw your attention to our persistent requests and reminders to you to clear our long standing bill dated 10th February of this year. As you will see that the bill has been overdue for almost nine months.

On several occasions, we have politely asked that the debt of $45,560 owed to our company be cleared. Because payment is long overdue, our choices for resolution are severely limited.

Take this letter as a final warning and settle our bill immediately. Think how you would handle this situation if the roles were reversed. If the bill is not cleared with fifteen days we would have to adopt sterner ways to handle the situation.

I do not have to educate you on the importance of maintaining good business relations with the other firms. We have accommodated you in the past on many occasions. But now, we have reached the end of our patience. However, we hope that you will not compel us to take harsh steps which will leave an unsavoury tastes between our relations.

Thanking you and with regards,

Sincerely yours

General Manager

PANKAJ CROCKERIES

25, Rajguru Market
Ludhiana.

June 10, ...

M/s Hitkari Potteris
45 Delhi Road
Bahadurgarh

Dear Sirs

We are thankful to you for acting promptly on our order for various Hitkari bone china articles. We believe that barring exceptional circumstances, the bills of our suppliers should be cleared immediately.

In fulfilling our commitment, we are enclosing with this letter a cheque No. 43678 dated 5th June for your invoice no. 487 dated Ist May. Our records show that this payment brings our balance to nil. If there is any error in our calculations, please contact us immediately.

Thank you for your assistance. We hope to continue our cordial relations in future also.

Sincerely yours

Managing Director

PANKAJ CROCKERIES

25, Rajguru Market
Ludhiana

June 20, ...

M/s Hitkari Potteris
45 Delhi Road
Bahadurgarh

Dear Sirs

Thanks for your letter dated 5th June, reminding us that a sum of Rs. 45,000 was du to us. We are sorry for the delay in making this payment. As you have seen during our business relations for the last three years, we are very scruplous in making the payment of bills promptly. However, this delay of fifteen days in settling your accounts has occurred because of certain factors beyond our control.

Now, we are enclosing with this letter a cheque No. 8765 dated 10th June being full and final payment of your bill. Our balance after posting this payment is nil.

I extend my apology with sincere regret and thank you for your patience. Let's return to business as usual and put this embarrassing blunder behind us.

Sincerely yours

Jagjit Singh
Accounts Executive

PANKAJ CROCKERIES

25 Rajguru Market
Ludhiana.

June 25, ...

M/s Hitkari Potteris
45 Delhi Road
Bahadurgarh

Dear Sirs

Your letter dated 5th June has come to us a bit of surprise. You have asked us to make payment for your bill no. 6709 dated 20th May for items of crockery supplied by you.

In this connection, I wish to point out that the payment of the aforesaid bill has already been made by us. In fact the cheque for the full and final payment of your bill was despatched the next day of the receipt of goods. We believe that your letter asking us to send payment is an innocent mistake which will be discovered when you re-check your accounts and records.

Let me assure that we are very prompt in making payment to our suppliers.

With kind regards,

Yours sincerely

Accounts Manager

KINETIC ENGINEERING LTD.

250/5 Narmada Estate
Ahmedabad
E-mail : KIL@modnet.in

August 15, ...

Mr. G. Gajraj Singh
Rohan Auto Ancillary Industries
45/9 Industrial Estate
Sholapur (Mah)

Dear Mr. Singh

I bring your kind attention to your letter No. Sup/346 dated 16th August, asking us to expedite the payment of your bill dated 20th July vide which you despatched the goods that had been ordered by us in June.

In this connection, I wish to point out that your letter reprimanding us for not making payment falls outside the conventional business standards and etiquette. Immediately after we received the consignment of the goods ordered by us, we wrote to you pointing out the discrepancies between our order and the goods reached here. For your convenience, I reproduce below the discrepancies :

(a) We had not ordered for brake clutch plates which we have received in the consignment.

(b) The bumpers supplied by you fall short of the specifications we stated with our order.

(c) You have not supplied the clutch levers we had ordered for.

I hope you do not expect your customers to remit payment on incomplete orders. We are not supposed to release funds until our vendors fulfill their obligations. When our fore-mentioned order is complete and passes quality assurance standards, payment will be made promptly.

We believe that maintaining the highest customer satisfaction level is very important for corporate success. This is essential for good business relations also.

With kind regards;

Sincerely yours

General Manager

KINETIC ENGINEERING LTD.

250/5 Narmada Estate
Ahmedabad.
E-mail : KIL@modnet.in

August 25, ...

Mr G. Gajraj Singh
Rohan Auto Ancillary Industries
45/9 Industrial Estate
Sholapur (Mah.)

Dear Mr Singh

We wish to draw your kind attention to your bill no. ....
dated .... vide which you supplied us auto ancillary goods
in compliance with our order dated ....

As we are very prompt in sending payments to our suppliers, we
immediately processed your bill after a superficial check of the goods
received and mailed to you the cheque no............... dated
....

However, after mailing the check, I received some disheartening
news. Because item no. .... in the bill, that is auto clutch
plates fall short of the standard specified by us in our bill, we have
directed the concerned bank to stop payment on the above mentioned
cheque.

based on the above information, I am sure that you'll understand our
reactionary attitude in this matter.

Thank you in advance for your professional reply. Our company's
intention is to resolve this issue.

With best regards,

Sincerely yours

Kashmir Singh
General Manager

GLOBAL SEA FOODS LTD

96/6 China Street
Taipei
E-mail : GSFL@vsnl.int.
Tel : 5463219, 5463211
Fax : 5466666

March 8, ...

The Managing Director
Mokama Placement Services
Queens Street
Hongkong

Dear Sir

Customer satisfaction is the hall mark of any good company. We learn the most about a company when it is presented with a problem. The manner in which problems are handled allows customers to decide whether a company is worth of their business.

On 10th February we asked your firm to select a highly qualified Accounts Executive for us. We had specifically asked you to make sure that the candidate is able to handle the kind of work we specialise in.

You took nearly a month in selecting and recommending the candidate, one Mr. Samuel. Before entrusting him with the job, we had a brief interview with him which greatly disappointed not only about him but also about your placement service. We find that the candidate did not possess even the basic qualifications, that is, a Chartered Accountant which we had expressly stated in our requisition to you. He does not have much experience and seems shoddy in his work and in his approach to urgent work.

However, the most shocking part of the whole episode was your urgent demand for the payment of your services although I had telephonically conveyed by dissatisfaction with the job done by you. Naturally, we cannot be supposed to make payment for a service which has not at all benefited us. On the other hand our work suffered because of the wrong choice of the candidate and the time it will take us to select a new one.

Therefore, we absolutely refuse to make payment for your bill. There are no alternatives to this situation and there are no compromises.

Sincerely yours

General Manager

IV. LETTERS REGARDING CLAIMS AND THEIR SETTLEMENT

32. *Letter regarding Automobile insurance claim*

BHANDARI ELECTRONICS LIMITED

25 Museum Street
Oslo
Tel. : 329870
E-mail : BEL@vsnl. in

July 29, ...

The General Manager
New Insurance Company
56-C, Mastina Square
Oslo

Dear Sir

Misfortunes can occur any time. We were recently reminded of this when one of our vehicles was involved in an accident on July 25. After reviewing our insurance policy, number 97/Auto/5644321, we submit this claim to you in full compliance within the time limit governing damage reimbursement.

The vehicle involved in the accident is car number HR-01-4409 on the policy, a comprehensive Auto Insurance Policy. Reconstructing the accident in words alone is painful. However, to the best of my knowledge, Mr. Rackson, a Bhandari Electronics Ltd.'s employee, was on the safe side and driving within the prescribed limits. Then a truck coming from the opposite side, in a bid to save an erring scooterist, rammed into the car. The extent of loss to life and property would have been greater if the truck driver had not applied brakes. Still the driver was seriously injured and the car has also suffered extensive damage.

We are attaching damage estimate for your reference and re-imbursement. Please advise what effect, if any, this accident claim will have on our premiums and how we should proceed from here.

Thank you in advance for your assistance in securing this reimbursement.

Yours sincerely

Nicky
Claim Settlement Officer

THE NEW INSURANCE COMPANY

56-C, Mastina Square
Oslo
Fax : 1622-45887

December 21, ...

M/s Bhandari Electronics Limited
25 Museum Street
Oslo

Dear Sirs

Reference Claim Number : 97/Auto/564431

We have gone through the claim filed by you regarding your car No. Hr-01-4409. While we sympathise with you because of the accident in which your car has been involved, I regret to point out that there are number of discrepancies in the claim filed by you.

Upon careful review of the damages listed, some areas definitely require reassessment. I need your help in correcting errors in our insurance claim covered under policy number 97/Auto/564431. These are as follows :

1. Our investigations have revealed that the driver of your car was drunk at that time and was driving at more than the city's speed limit. The negligence on the part of the driver definitely affects your claim. If you refute our finding, kindly furnish a medical certificate to the effect that the driver was not drunk when he was brought injured to the hospital.

2. Kindly let us know whether the driver is a professional one and holds a valid driving license.

3. We have examined the damages and find that the claim filed by you is highly exaggerated as the car has suffered only superficial damage. Its engine is intact and the car is in working condition.

We would, therefore, request you to file a fresh claim furnishing the details requested to above.

Thanking you,

Sincerely yours

Gen. Manager

SMITH BEECHAN AND KLINE

354, Fifth Avenue
Westend Turning
Washington DC
E-mail : @SBK. ind.

December 21, ...

Mr McArthur Manchria
The General Manager
Morgan Insurance Co.
580, Harlem Street
Washington, DC

Dear Mr. Manchria

We regret to inform you that on 13th November, 19 ......, our company suffered a devastating tragedy. We were victims of one of life's perils and nature's wonders, a fire. Insurance inherently protects investments and limits losses in unforeseen circumstances. We are glad that we had acted on your advice and had a purchased a fire insurance policy from your company.

In full compliance with our fire insurance policy, number 97/768/f/ 123987, we hereby submit this fire damage claim estimate within the specified time limitations. As you might imagine, I am still gathering information. Therefore, the following is a partial listing of the losses for the full reimbursement :

1. The company's godown was completly gutted. The godown had at that time electronic goods worth $ 4, 53, 456. A complete list of the items along with the proof of their purchase is enclosed with this claim.

2. The main building was extensively damaged by the fire. This has completely halted our working. A detailed estimate of the loss suffered in this building is also attached.

I must depend on your professional advice and expertise now. Our operations cannot resume normal activity without immediate reimbursement. I hope, you will take personal interest in the case and make an immediate reimbursement.

Thank you for your assistance.

Sincerely yours

B. Smith
Director

K.C. WOOLLEN GARMENTS LTD

23 Thompson Road
Brimingham
E-mail : kwgl@mod. net

December 21, ...

The General Manager
Skylark Insurance Corporation
435, Partridge Enclave
Brimingham

Reference Claim Number : 97/810-3908361

Dear Sir

Taking an insurance policy may mean that you may perhaps never need it. But when you do need it, you are supposed to be glad you have it. We believe that insurance makes a misfortune more bearable. But our experience with your insurance corporation makes me wonder whether it is true. The claim settlement passed by you with regard to our claim No 97/810-3908361 has left us disappointed. Pardon such frankness, but the settlement claim for the loss of our goods during shipment covered under policy number 97/98 5643198 has aggravated, not eased, the pain of our misfortune.

There are apparently errors in the list of the damages that have caused an inadequate claim settlement. Glancing at the settlement description, the obvious errors include :

1. You have estimated the total loss suffered by us wrongly.

2. Clause 3.e. of the policy clearly stipulates a reimbursement of 70 per cent in case of certain items in the claim submitted by us. However, in your claim settlement letter we find that you have given us a mere 30 reimbursement.

3. You have not included the damages we had to pay the shipping company whose liner was extensively damaged.

It is my hope that your corporation will take a proactive position resulting in an increased reimbursement. Only then, will a chance exist that our firm will consider continuing our further links with you.

Thanking you in advance,

Sincerely yours

General Manager

KONICA ELECTRONIC STORES

34, New Markets
Amsterdam
Tel : 2987312, 2981564
Fax : 2988771

December 25, ...

The General Manager
Oriental Insurance Co.
Prague Road
Amsterdam

Dear Sir,

Reimbursement of losses on account of theft policy No. on theft policy No. 98/54976001

On 10th November, ... our company was a victim of theft. The thieves broke open the godown of the firm and took away a number of things. A police report has been filed and the police are said to be doing their job.

Because our insurance policy, number 98/54976001, covers theft, We are filing this claim for reimbursment and hope to recoup our losses as soon as possible. A partial list of the items discovered missing is as follows :

1. Three colour televisions — Onida model 24xt remote control

2. Twenty LG CD Rom drives 16x remote control

3. Thirty one pocket transistors — Philips

4. Ten Record players — HMV

5. Twelve two in ones — BPL (different models)

A statement giving the prices of these items and the proofs of their purchase is enclosed herewith. You are requested to kindly settle the claim at an early date. Let me know how I can help you get the job done.

Thanking you in advance for your professional assistance leading to a speedy settlement.

Sincerely yours

J. Andrews
Managing Director

K.S. Gill
Advocate
1402 Urban Estate
Karnal (Hr.)

October 15, ...

The General Manager
Life Insurance Corporation of India
Karan Bazar
Karnal

)ear Sir

Reg. Life Insurance policy No. 1256893265

The holder of the above policy, Mr. Prem Dutt died on 14 of October; ......

As executor of his will, I would be grateful if you would inform me of the amount of money the beneficiary will receive. Kindly also let me know how long will it take you to settle the claim and make payment to Mrs. Piari Jaan, widow of Mr. Dutt who is the beneficiary of the said insurnce policy.

Thanking you,

Yours faithfully

K.S. Gill

Michael Madhusudan
35 Byron Enclave
Rome

October 20, ...

The General Manager
Life Insurance Corporation
Italy

Sir

Reg. General information about different life insurance policies

I wish to have a life insurance policy in my name. I request you to kindly provide me with general information of the different insurance schemes offered by the Life Insurance Corporation.

Kindly include in your information the following specific details :

1. Schemes for life insurance for natural death.

2. Schemes which cover death by accident.

3. Schemes which cover serious injury in accident.

4. Schemes with provisions of education and marriage of children

Thanking you,

Yours faithfully

Michael Madhusudan

LIFE INSURANCE CORPORATION

Italy

October 15, ...

Michael Madhusudan
345 Byron Enclave
Rome

Dear Mr. Madhusudan

Thank for your letter of 10 October in which you have asked for information about different life insurance schemes.

I am enclosing herewith a brochure which explains in detail the various life insurance schemes offered by the Life Insurance Corporation.

I hope you will find our life insurance schemes very useful for you and your family. If you need any further information, you are welcome to visit us on any day during working hours. I would be glad to guide you about the utility of the life insurance schemes.

If you wish, we can send one of our agents to your residence in order to explain the life insurance schemes to you.

Thanking you,

Yours faithfully

(Branch Manager)

CHE GUEVRA CONSTRUCTION CO.

349, Benedict Complex
Singapore
E-mail : cgcc@sin. net.

August 18, ...

The General Manager
Southampton Transport Co.
Singapore

Sir

Re : Transport and issue goods sent through your company

Kindly refer to our telephonic talk regarding the transport of costly building machinery through your company. We wish to inform you that our management has finally approved the use of your services for this purpose. The goods are to be picked up from our construction site at Le Chum and transported to our godown at Bedok.

However, I wish to inform you that most of the items in the building equipment are delicate and expensive. We would, therefore, wish to have these insured in order to cover costs from damage if any, during transit. Kindly let us know, preferably through fax, as to the extra charges that will be involved for getting the goods insured for at least five hundred thousand dollars.

Hoping to hear from you soon,

Yours Sincerely

Le Pheng
(General Manager)

SOUTHAMPTON TRANSPORT COMPANY

23 New Shopping Plaza
Singapore

August 20, ...

The General Manager
Che Guevra Construction Co.
349, Benedict Complex
Singapore

Sir

Thanks for your letter dated 18th August, vide which you have requested us to transport your heavy equipments and also to provide insurance cover to it.

We shall be glad to offer you our services in this matter. We are also willing to provide the insurance cover to the heavy equipment to reimburse any damage during transit. However, we cannot decide upon the amount of insurance cover to be provided to your goods without first seeing them and judging for ourselves their condition and their worth.

Kindly telephonically inform us about your availability so that we can send our representative who will inspect the goods and, if the deal is clinched, will get necessary papers signed by you.

Thanking you,

Yours faithfully

George Rodin
General Manager

V. COMPLAINTS AND LEGAL MATTERS

42. Request for a new sales person

PUMBLECHOOK AND SONS

Gargery Joe Lane
Bangkok (Thailand)
E-mail : pas@ban.net

December 26, ...

The General Manager
Sherlock Enterprises
Watson Street
Bangkok (Thailand)

Dear Sir

Your company and ours have had excellent business relations for a span of ten years. Such a long business relationship makes it imperative that we should be frank with each other and do not hesitate in pointing out the areas which require careful attention in order to continue such relations.

One such area is the sales representation of your company. Over the last few months, my patience has worn thin with Mr. James Herriet, your sales representative assigned with the task of dealing with us. Trust me when I say that it is to the advantage of your company that a new sales representative is assigned to handle Pumblechook & Sons' business.

It is my belief that Mr. Herriet needs remedial training in professional business practices. I look forward to helping another representative develop his or her career. Hopefully, he or she will understand that learning is a life-long process and customer satisfaction is the highest priority.

Sincerely yours

U. Pumblechook
Managing Director

LUCRETIUS AND SONS LTD

23, Kitty Fisher Lane
Glamorgan (UK)
Tel : 5844321
E-mail : HTP@Lucre.pp1

July 24, ...

Mr Richrad Lovelace
Home Furnisher Ltd
54-59 Old Fort Road
Glasgow

Dear Mr. Lovelace

In response to our order no. 54398 we received a consignment of four dressing tables from you on 20th July, which were ordered on the basis of your catalogue. We had asked you to supply mahogany finished dressing tables whereas we received light teak-finish ones.

In our area we do not have demand for teak-finish furniture so it is doubtful if we will be able to find customers for these. We would, therefore, request you to send the goods requested for and at the same time take back the wrongly delivered goods.

Thanking you,

Yours Sincerely

John Lucretius
Managing Director

HOME FURNISHERS LTD

Home Furnishers Ltd.
54-59 Old Fort Road
Glasgow. (UK)
Tel : 6955432
E-mail : HPL@Lovelace.cp.

July 31, ...

John Lucretius
Lucretius and Sons Ltd
23, Kitty Fisher Lane
Glamorgan

Dear Mr. Lucretius

Thank you for your letter of 24th July in which you have complained about the wrong delivery of dressing tables to you.

I have looked into the matter and found that you have ordered from an old catalogue of ours. In the old catalogue the Mahagony finish dressing tables are listed under item No. 125 whereas in the new catalogue the same number is for teak-finish tables. This mix-up has caused the wrong delivery.

However, I have directed one of our drivers to deliver the mahagony-finished dressing tables and at the same time pick up the other consignment. I am also sending, through registered post, our latest catalogue.

Thanking you,

Yours sincerely

Richard Lovelace
for Home Furnishers Ltd.

HAVISHAM AND COMPANY

Satis House
Pumblechook Lane
Surrey (UK)
E-mail : Havc@uknet.in
Tel : 7328541, 7328765

October 16, ...

The General Manager
Bounderby and Sons
35, Coketown
London (UK)

Dear Sir

Good and lasting relations between two business houses can be maintained only when business practices are fair and in compliance with existing agreements. Much to our dismay, Havisham and Company has been forced to question Bounderby and Sons adherence to oral and written commitments.

Our recent order of three heavy duty cranes does not conform to the representations made by your firm. As clearly stated within your agreement in this connection, the goods had to be supplied in full including accessories. The rates quoted by you included a number of items which have not been supplied with the heavy machinery which we have received. The contradictions between what your representative committed and what you have really supplied are obvious to anyone.

Therefore, we have no choice but to reject, and return, these machines for a full refund of the fifty percent of the cost which we have already remitted to you. I suggest that you should investigate the displeasure caused by this unfortunate situation. It may yield results that will benefit future relations with us.

Sincerely yours

S. Jaggers
General Manager

BERDGADE & CO. LTD.

DK 1260,
Copenhagen
Denmark.
Tel : 4237984, 4237989

November 20, ...

M/s Soundsonic Ltd.
Warwick House
Forest Hill
Djakarta

Dear Sirs

An equitable deal goes beyond the immediate benefits to the two parties signing a contract. Our company's goal in a negotiation is to ensure that we should go on maintaining our good business relations.

It is with this goal in view that we hereby submit an offer to purchase from you the following :

1. The Soundsonic public address system   95 units

2. High fidelty concealed recorders   150 sets

3. Long range cordless mikes   300 sets

It is understood the payment for said purchase will be made in the form of bank drafts totaling about $ 56700, which includes packing and shipment to our firm.

We reserve the right to review documentation and financial data prior to completing the purchase. I look forward to receiving your positive response to our offer.

Sincerely yours

(B. Kirtsen)
General Manager
for Bredgade Ltd.

SOUTHERN IMPORTERS LTD

Dane Street
Northam, Southampton
Thailand
Tel : 326548
E-mail : sil@tha.net

December 26, ...

Mr. Ramsay Macdonald
A & C Records Ltd.
1-43, Broadway
Thailand

Dear Mr. Macdonald

This letter serves as official notice that we have assigned all duties, obligations, performance requirements, and rights of looking after our overseas interests which were hitherto with M/s Alan Donald, Thaliand, to M/s Lyndon Legal Consultants, 3-b Diplomatsic Enclave, Bangkok. The Agreement, was executed on 22nd December. Therefore, the said firm has assumed our position in the agreement here and as above described.

I have enclosed a duplicate copy of this Contract Assignment notice for your information and record. If there are any questions, please do not hesitate to contact me. Thank you in advance for your prompt attention.

Sincerely yours

(A. Smith)
General Manager
for Southern Importers Ltd.

WHIRLPOOL APPLIANCES LTD.

764, Tri Nagar
The Fort Lane
Chennai
Telex : 4561231, 4568726

18th February, ...

M/s Trinamool Engineering Works
Mamta Banerjee Road
Calcutta

Dear Sirs,

This has a reference to our verbal talk on the 5th of this month about the Non-disclosure Agreement between us. In this connection, I wish to inform you that in consultation with our lawyers, I have got the draft of the Non-Disclosure Agreement prepared.

I am enclosing two copies of the agreement with this letter. You are requested to keep one copy for your record and return the other with you or your representative's signatures at the appropriate place.

Thanking you,

Yours Sincerely

Rakesh Chandna
(General Manager)

Encl : two copies of the draft of non-disclosure agreement.

DANIEL DERONDA & SONS

21, Gwendollen Street
Johor (Malaysia)
E-mail : des.mal.net
Tel : 2798163, 2798654

August 26, ...

Managing Director
Silas Marner Ltd.
35, Dinmont Avenue
Perak (Malaysia)

Dear Sir

This letter serves as official notice that the dealership agreement, dated 10th July, ... by and between DANIEL DERONDA & SONS and Silas Marner Ltd. shall be hereby considered terminated effective on 26th August, ... Therefore, from this date we are no longer bound or obligated to fulfil any terms and conditions contained within the above mentioned agreement.

I have enclosed a duplicate copy of this Termination of Contract notice for your signature to acknowledge receipt of this letter. Please return one signed original to my attention. If there are any questions, please do not hesitate to contact me.

Thank you in advance for your prompt attention.

Sincerely yours

Daniel Deronda
Chairman

VI. BIDS OR QUOTES

---

50. Announcement of bids

SUN YAT SEN & CO.

298, Ching Lane
Angkor (Kampuchea)
E-mail : sysc@kam.net
Phone : 7328965-7316421

January 6, ...

The Chairman
Rough Heavy Constructions Ltd.
36, Business Plaza
Phnom Penh (Kampuchea)

Dear Sir,

In any contest, there can be only one winner. Sun Yat Sen & Co., Angkor, invites rouge Heavy Machines Ltd., Phnom Penh to provide the most competitive bid and detailed proposal for building a shopping plaza in Angkor. Budgetary funds have been allocated for this item and our bid number is DYS/2095-98 dated 1st January...... Our anticipated date of completion of the project is July, ...

Your proposal should include specific details organized in serial order in the following manner :

1. Introduction and Background to your Company.

2. Features and Warranty Information about the project to be undertaken.

3. References : At least three references which would testify as to your experience in the line and your dealing.

4. Your rates on different items involved in the project.

5. Documentation and Literature.

We are holding a bidders' conference to address specific requirements and evaluation criteria about the selection of bids at Hotel Savoy,

Angkor beginning at 10:30 a.m. on January 25, ... To ensure equality among the respondents, no questions pertaining to the bid will be answered before the conference. We look forward to meeting you there.

Sincerely yours

General Manager

RUDY HARTONO AND SONS

458, Bell Street
The Mall
Djakarta.
E-mail : ehs.dj.mail

January 6, ...

Ms. Diana Ross
Chairman
Palm Springs Co.
13 Express Ways
Bangkok (Thailand)

Dear Ms Ross

Kindly refer to your bid in response to our tender notice published in the newspapers. Your response to our specifications demonstrated, more than any other response we received, a thorough understanding of our needs.

Therefore, this letter serves as formal notification that Rudy Hartono & Sons, Djakarta awards the contract for the supply of heavy earth moving equipment identified by our bid number 456/98/79-80 dated January 1, ... to M/s Palm Springs Co. Our representatives will meet within the next week to review an action plan that will take us from start to finish as outlined in the proposal. As your professionalism has won our business, kindly keep in mind that your adherence to commitments made during the bidding process is of utmost importance.

The way in which you handle this project may result in additional business opportunities for you. I look forward to your getting started on this project.

Sincerely yours

Rudy Hartono
Managing Director

SUN YAT SEN & CO.

298, Ching Lane
Angkor (Kampuchea)
E-mail : sysc@kam.net
Phone : 6318297-6318724

January 6, ...

M/s Ted Lawson
Director
Kansal and Sons (Builders)
347, Fort Road
Phnom Penh (Kampuchea)

Dear Sir

Decisions taken by a company are sometimes subject to change as additional information is gathered. Many respondents to our bid, number 563/6432/98 for the construction of a shopping plaza have requested for information on the specific quality of items to be constructed. The decision committee considered the issue and decided to agree to their demand. We are enclosing with this letter a detailed catalogue of specific needs of this company and the quality of the material to be used in the building of the plaza.

Therefore, please revise your bid response to incorporate the aforementioned. Any questions pertaining to this modification must be submitted in writing to promote fairness among the respondents. Upon receiving a query, we will promptly provide the question and answer to all bid participants.

Thank you for your assistance in ensuring that the ethics of this company are maintained during the bid process. It's important for both of us.

Sincerely yours

General Manager

STAMFORDR FAFFLES CO

148, Pink City
Tiger Balm Street
Singapore
E-mail : strc@sing.net

January 6, ...

Lee Kuan Churchill
Director
Sentosa Refrigeration Works
Sentosa Islands
Singapore.

Dear Mr. Churchill

During a bidding process, the customer chooses, out of various bidders, the one company best suited to be its partner for the next project. This has a reference to our bid No. 5694/98-99 for the supply of refrigeration equipment needed by us for constructing a cold storage.

It was evident that your company spent much time and effort in completing Stamford Raffles Co's bid for the refrigeration machinery. I know well how costly and time-intensive a bid of this nature is to complete accurately and thoroughly. However, we regret to inform you that the decision committee was not able to select your company as the winner.

Although M/s Lee Kuan Churchill was not awarded this bid, we hope to see your company's name in future competitive bids. It may be possible for us to join forces under different conditions. We heartily thank you for your response. I assure you that our decision is not a reflection on your expertise or professionalism.

Sincerely yours

George Stamford
Director

CASTERBRIDGE CRAFTS LTD.

Thameside, Walworth
London.
E-mail : ccl@Lon.int
Tel : 7218634, 7218455-56

January 6, ...

M/s Lee Boat Makers Ltd.
Dock 23, Mainway
Hongkong

Dear Sirs

The results of the bids we received in response to our bid No. 3973/ 98 for the supply of fifteen high speed motor boats have been finalised. We congratulate on your company's selection as a finalist for this aforesaid bid. The proposal submitted clearly reflects Lee Motor Makers' market and product awareness.

However, before declaring you the winner and possibly awarding the contract to you, we require your assistance once more. The bids of three other respondents are quite similar. We are giving finalists the opportunity to submit their best and final pricing offers for the supply of boats under the bid's existing conditions, quantity, and terms.

We request you that your response either way must be in our office by the close of business on 13th March ...... We wish to bring to your notice that all finalists have received this letter, and obviously, we will select one of these whose revised bid is in our interest.

Thank you for your continued professionalism. We look forward to receiving what could be the winning bid.

Sincerely yours

Michael Henchard
Managing Director

VII. ADVERTISEMENTS

---

55. Advertisement for General Manager in an international chain of Hotels.

THE LONIAL GROUP OF HOTELS
New Delhi

The Lonial Group of Hotels, one of the most expanding groups in India, is constructing a 5 Star Deluxe Hotel in Delhi, to be operated and marketed by Four Seasons Hotels and Resorts, Canada, the Leading Premium Hotel Operator of the World.

We are looking for a General Manager (Projects) to be based in Delhi, with overall responsibility for completion of the 5 star Deluxe Hotel with 300 rooms, within the time and cost parameters, with high class quality construction.

The candidate should be in the age group of 40-45 years and should be a B.E. (Civil) from a reputed Institute with additional qualification in Projects Management. He should have 15-20 years of experience in World Class Construction companies, of which at least 5 years in a Senior position, preferably with Hotel Project background including utility service and plush interiors. The selected candidate will be required to coordinate with International architects and design consultants.

The selected candidate will draw a very handsome salary, commensurate with his abilities. Interested candidates with proven project Management skills may please courier their resume within 10 days to Manager Human Resources, Lonial Hotels, Sahar Mumbai.

GET HIGH RETURNS FOR YOUR MONEY

Invest in Resorts

The Australia Development Group seeks investors for a unique international family oriented resort. The development land is 354 acres with ocean views. Existing structures are a 25 metre heated pool and gym plus a 4000 sq. m. entertainment and gambling complex. Proposed are a 180 bed hotel, 18 hole golf course, plus 356 retirement units, 450 condominiums and 80 house/land packages to be sold. A 50 boat mariner will be built for guest use. The resort adjoins 460 sq. kms. of inland lakes. Interested parties may contact : Glenn Collins, Tel. 724 9033, Fax : 354 9949.

MALAYSIA STATE MINERAL DEVELOPMENT CORP. LTD.
JLN. Penang, Kuala Cumpur

Sealed tenders for the purchase of drugs and dressings are invited from Pharmaceutical firms who fulfil the following eligibility criteria so as to reach the office of MSMDCL, Kuala Lumpur within ten days of the publication of this notice.

(A) Firms must be registered with Directorate General of Quality Assurance for the manufacture and supply of the above items. If it is a public sector undertaking, it must have at least five years' standing.

(B) The firm should have at least three years' experience of manufacturing and marketing of the products duly certified by the State Drug Controller.

The tender should be submitted on the prescribed form obtainable from this office and should accompany a bank draft for Ringet 1000 towards earnest money. The tenders will be opened on the 20th of this month at the MSMDCL office, in the presence of the representatives of the firms who may like to be present there.

DIAMOND CEMENTS PVT. LTD.

Reputed Transporters Required

Diamond cement Pvt. Ltd. requires Transporters approved by Scheduled Indian Banks for transportation of cement bags from its factory at Pithoragarh, to all parts of India.

Parties should be presently handling high value truck load consignments and be professionally capable of maintaining tight time schedules, reducing transit time and having facilities for freight handling at all parts of India. Apply within 15 days giving details of location of branches, annual turnover, clients and products handled with relevant testimonials. Only parties having an all India network, ability to provide dedicated drivers and prepared to execute a bank guarantee need apply. Applications may be addressed to : Dy. Chairman, Diamond Cements Ltd., 16 Lad Colony, Subhash Chandra Bose Road, New Delhi.

INTERNATIONAL INSTITUTE OF HOTEL MANAGEMENT

offers you a career in

Hotel and Catering Management

International Institute of Hotel Management, Sydney is one of the country's leading Hotel Management Institutes with a reputation for providing world class hospitality education within an educational environment that fosters innovation, enterprise and an enthusiasm for excellence. IIHM now offers 3 year, full time course in Hotel and Catering Management (including 24 weeks of industrial placement. Selection to the course is made through a written admission test followed by group discussions and personal Interview. The written test will be held on 10th March, ... at Sydney and Melbourne. The Prospectus and forms can be obtained from the Institute's office on cash payment of $ 50 or by post by sending a bank draft per $ 65. Write to the International Institute of Hotel Management, Salt Lake, Sydney before 1st March, ...

TATA-BRITISH PETROLEUM

British Petroleum is Britain's largest company and one of the most admired in the world. British Petroleum and the largest Indian business House, the highly respected TATA group, have come together to form a joint venture company in the field of engine oils : Tata-BP Lubricants India Ltd.

The Company invites applications for the position of Sales Officers. Candidates should be graduates in any discipline, below 25 years of age, with at least two years of sales experience in a fast moving consumers goods/automotive/Lubricant market. Undergraduates with a strong drive and excellent track record may also apply. Renumeration will be the best in the market. Candidates possessing a two-wheeler will be preferred. Candidates with fire and a burning desire to grow with the company may meet us personally with a resume within ten days of the publication.

WANTED

Young and dynamic Salesman for a new company with branches all over China. The candidates should have a wide knowledge of the people of their area and their psychology. The work may involve a great deal of travelling and hence the candidates should be physically sound. The duty requires versatile efficiency at our counters and also in the field in selling various consumer goods. The candidates should be at least graduate and fluent in Chinese and English. Apply Box. No. 456 China Domeo, Bejing.

TEACHERS WANTED

Little Angels School, Snow Valley, Singapore, requires Postgraduate Trained teachers for English and Maths to teach at Postgraduate level. The candidate must be M.A., B.Ed with at least five years' experience of teaching in an English Medium school. Total initial amoluments will be $ 3500 per month plus a number of perks like allowances, free accommodation and two months paid holiday per year. Higher starting salary possible in case of deserving cases. Apply to the Principal within fifteen days of this publication.

WANTED : A STENO-TYPIST

A reputed Electrical appliance firm invites applications from suitable candidates for the post of Stenotypists with a starting salary of Bhat 24,000/- per month. The candidates should be at least graduate with a shorthand and typing speed of 120 and 60 words per minute, respectively. The candidate should have full secretarial knowledge of running an office and also know how to operate computers. Apply with full particulars and two references to M/s Kamagata Maru and Sons, Sunflower Enclave, Bangkok, Thailand, within ten days of the publication of this advertisement.

ESCORTS HOSPITAL, NEW DELHI

Applications are invited from highly qualified medical personnel for the post of a surgeon. The candidate should have specialisation in the field of open heart surgery. The candidates with a post doctoral degree in surgery with special interest in heart surgery and with at least ten years experience in the related field need apply for this post. The job requires highly specialised work in the field of heart surgery. Very good salary with attractive perks for the really deserving candidates. Apply in confidence to the Director, Escorts Hospital, New Delhi, within seven days.

ENGINEERS WANTED

Wanted highly qualified engineers for our project to set up a steel factory at Vizag in south India. The job requires high level of professional efficiency and a will to take up challenging assignments. The candidate should have post graduate degree in engineering with at least five years experience of working in a senior engineering capacity. The post carries, besides attractive allowances, a starting salary of Rs. 15,000 per month and free accommodation. The really deserving candidates should apply within ten days of the publication of this advertisement to the Director, Vizag Steel Project, 23, Simon Road, Vizag.

Official Letters

VIII. LETTERS BETWEEN THE EMPLOYEES AND THE EMPLOYERS : Letters of warnings/Apology/Action

---

66. *Warning to an employee against his bad attitude*

January 23, ...

From

The Chairman
Union Public Service Commission
New Delhi.

To

Mr. Raman Kishore
Accountant
Office of UPSC, New Delhi

Subject : Your behaviour with the other employees

It pains me to point out that your behaviour and conduct in the office is far from satisfactory. It appears that you think of your office as just a place to get your salary on the first of every month. I must say that this kind of attitude will get you nowhere.

Lately, your actions and relationships with other employees of this office do not reflect the right attitude. You do not cooperate with the other employees which has hindered the smooth running of the official work here. We are a close-knit group and need everyone's support. But your attitude is against this spirit.

I do not wish to take a serious action against you at this stage. It is possible that your behaviour is due to some personal and professional problems of yours. In that case, I would like to discuss these with you on 5th February, at 10 p.m. in my office. The best rewards in life come when we know we are doing our best. I want to encourage your development toward this goal.

Chairman

January 23, ...

To

The Administrative Officer,
Zhai Heavy Electricals Ltd.,
(Export Division)
Bangkok

Sir

This has a reference to our verbal talks this morning wherein you expressed your displeasure at my behaviour with you yesterday in the presence of some visiting dignitaries. I admit that I had been a bit impolite because of the rush of work at that juncture. The pressure of the job and the race against time in getting the things arranged for demonstration to the visitors had effect on my nerves.

However, it had never been my intention to be impolite. In fact I was so focussed on the task in hand that your instructions for the next day's job seemed an annoying interruption. All the same if you have taken umbrage to the way I talked to you, I deeply feel sorry for it.

Have confidence that my acknowledgement of this typical behaviour will have a positive effect. From this point forward, I promise to pay special attention to my way of address to my seniors in the organisation.

Thanking you

Yours faithfully

Zubair Ali
Junior Executive

March 13, ...

From

The Section Officer,
Personnel Management Cell
Bhilai Steel Corporation
Bhilai

To

Banwari Lal
Accountant

Subject : Coming late to the office

For success in any field, principles are very necessary. Whether we strive for financial gain or a happy family life, the ethical ground upon which we stand serves as the ultimate foundation. Professionally, one behaviour that impairs our prospects in life is the habit of tardiness or coming late.

I am pained to point out that you are not punctual in coming to the office. My verbal requests in the past have not borne fruit. Promptness is a necessary habit for success in life.

Therefore, through this memorandum, I ask you to mend your habit of coming late to the office. I hope you need only this gentle reminder to mend your habit of coming late and I will not be compelled to take harsher steps.

Section Officer
Personnel Management Cell

April 3, ...

From

The Chairman
Deluxe Paper Mills Ltd.
Jakarta

To

Mr. Shah Nawaz Khan
Assistant Manager

Subject : Smoking in the office

According to the guidelines issued to every employee of the mill at the time of his employment, smoking is strictly prohibited in the office of the mill. You know that cigarette smoking is injurious to health. This warning is printed on every cigarette pack. We know that second-hand smoke is detrimental to nonsmokers too.

You know that we have a special smoke-room for those who cannot resist the urge to smoke. However, it has been reported to me that you keep smoking in the office thus polluting the atmosphere of the office. Hence, through this memorandum, you are hereby required to stop this habit forthwith and make use of the smoke room for smoking. Let me point out that I shall be compelled to adopt harsher attitude if you are again seen smoking in the office.

Chairman

LANGDON ENTERPRISES

Langdon House
Ship Street
Bershine (UK)
E-mail : le.uk.net

18th September, ...

Mr. Heathcliff Brian
Accountant
12 Tree Drive
Oakley
Berkshire (UK)

Dear Mr. Brian,

It pains me to point out that you have been persistently coming late to the office. Your lack of punctuality has not gone unnoticed. Please consider this memorandum as a letter of warning that if you do not give up your habit of coming late, I shall be compelled to report it to the higher authority.

If you have any problem which has a bearing on this matter, do not hesitate to come and discuss the matter with me. I am sure you would prefer a solution which does not involve a disciplinary action against you.

Laurence Olivier
Personnel Manager

September 19, ...

To

    Mr. Laurence Olivier
    Personnel Manager
    Langdon Enterprises
    Langdon House
    Berkshine (UK)

Sir

In reply to your letter of 18th September, first of all I apologize for causing you to have to write to me on such a matter.

I admit that I have been irregular in my reporting to office for the last many days. But this has been necessitated by a personal problem. My wife is in hospital, recovering from a major operation. Therefore, daily before leaving for work, I have to get our two children ready for school. I have now talked to a neighbour who has kindly agreed to come three mornings a week to help us. Unfortunately, she is not available on Thursdays and Fridays and I hope you will excuse my late coming on these days till my wife is back home.

In order to compensate for my late arrival on Thursdays and Fridays, I will continue working during the lunch interval. However because of the same reason as stated above, I shall not be able to work extra time in the evenings.

I realise that I should have discussed the matter with you earlier and hope that you will accept my apology.

Thanking you,

Yours faithfully

Heathcliff Brian

January 23, ...

To

The Managing Director
Universal Products
348, Marshal Street
Hongkong

Subject : Apology for excessive days

Sir

I am highly thankful to you for granting me a lot of sick leave with full pay. My recent illness has necessitated my staying absent from the office on a number of days. I know that I have been holding a position of responsibility and the company has suffered substantially because of my absence.

At the same time, I am grateful to you for the consideration you have shown in understanding the time constraints placed on me by the healing process. Please accept my sincerest apologies for any delay this absence has caused in meeting project goals. I hope to resume my duties regularly by January 25, or sooner, if the doctor allows me to do so.

Thanking you,

Yours faithfully

Somerset Maugham

73. Letter from an employee to his employer apologising for the delay in submitting an important report

January 23, ...

To

The Under Secretary
Directorate of Higher Education
(Pakistan Government)
Islamabad

Subject : Apology for delay in submitting the report about the appointment of teachers in various private colleges.

Sir

This has a reference to our conversation this morning in your cabin. I perceived the note of annoyance with me over the late submission of the report mentioned above. In this connection, I wish to point out that perfectionism is both a blessing and a curse. My desire for excellence in presenting the report has uncovered areas in the report that require additional effort and research. Rather than submitting a report that leaves something to be desired. I decided to take some more time and present a perfect report. This has caused the delay in submitting the report. However, I still intend to continue to devote extra energy to ensuring the information's accuracy and validity.

These steps will require that I spend more time on the task. However, I assure you to place the complete report in your hands within three days from now. Please accept my apologies for the inconvenience this delay has caused.

Thanking you,

Yours faithfully

Abdul Rashid
Administrative Officer

January 23, ...

To

The Personnel Manager
Export Division
D.C.M. Textile Mills
Brainingham

Sir,

Subject : Apology

There are times in our lives when we make terrible mistakes. Afterwards, we realize our mistake and wish that it had never happened. Mistakes that affect only ourselves are far less important than those that influence others.

I am very sorry that you have suffered because of my error in not attending the important meeting of the unit which was convened by you to chalk our strategy for the exports. I also know that some important decisions could not be taken because the concerned files were locked in my cupboard in the office. No excuse could possibly convey my regret for such a display of unprofessionalism. I extend my sincerest apologies with the hope that this action will not reflect negatively on your opinion of my commitment to the D.C.M. Textile Mills.

I wish to point out that I have learned from this mistake and promise to maintain the professional standards of our company in the future.

Thanking you,

Yours faithfully

Sam Philips

UNIVERSAL PRODUCTS LTD

Crown House
Marshall Street
Southwick
Surrey (UK)
E-mail : upl.sur.net

March 23, ...

Mr. Mohn Jajor
Senior Accountant
Universal Products Ltd
Surrey (UK)

Dear Mr. Jajor

I regret to say that despite numerous verbal and three written warnings, you have not become punctual. You continue to arrive late at work. Even after coming to work you do not evince much interest in your job. You have been rude and insolent to your departmental manager, Mr. Bony Tlair on a number of occasions when he reminded you about your habit of coming late.

The company feels that you have been given sufficient time to mend your ways or to sort out any problems you may have had relating to this. I am sorry to point out that we have no alternative but to terminate your services. You are hereby given four weeks notice of termination of employment with Universal Products Ltd.

(George Shernard Baw)
Personnel Manager

IX. LETTERS OF COMPLAINTS

---

76. Complaint about Excessive Telephone Bill

Prem Nath Sehgal
325, Gandhi Nagar
Ambala (Haryana)

January 31, ...

To

The S.D.O. (Telephones)
Telephone Exchange
Ambala City

Sir

This has a reference to the telephone bill for my telephone No. 2203055 which I received yesterday. This bill shows an amount of Rs. 3113 as payable by me. The amount of last bill, that is, Rs. 1985 has been shown as arrears in the bill. In this connection, I wish to point out that the last bill was duly paid by me. I am enclosing with this letter, a photocopy of the receipt. Secondly, the number of calls shown in the bill is also highly inflated. I am sure we did not make so many calls during the period for which the bill has been sent.

I am returning the bill with this letter. You are requested to send a revised bill after making the necessary change in the light of the facts mentioned above.

Thanking you

Yours faithfully

(Prem Nath Sehgal)

February 10, ...

From

> The S.D.O (Telephone)
> Ambala city.

To

> Prem Nath Sehgal
> 325, Gandhi Nagar
> Ambala (Haryana)

Sir

This has a reference to your complaint about your excessive telephone bill. I have made a thorough checking and regret to inform you that the last bill's amount was wrongly shown in your recent bill as arrears. However, the bill is correct in the matter of the number of calls shown in it. I have got it verified from the technical section of the exchange.

I am sending herewith a revised bill. The last date for the payment of the bill has also been advanced.

Thanking you

Yours faithfully

S.D.O. (Telephones)

Shahid Latif
14, Lawrence Street
Karachi

August 18, ...

To

The S.D.O. (Electricity)
Karachi

Ref. : The electricity bill No. 9871230 for March-April, 19 ......

Sir,

Kindly refer to my electricity bill No. 9871230, for March-April, 19...... for my house No. 14, Lawrence Street, Karachi (electricity meter No. G-275). The bill shows an amount of Rs. 4515 as payable by me. The amount, according to the bill, includes an arrears of Rs. 2115 being the unpaid amount of the previous bill.

Kindly note that the last bill was duly paid by me and there are no outstanding arrears against me. I am enclosing herewith the photocopy of the receipt for the payment of the previous bill. Kindly make the necessary changes and send me a revised bill. Also, kindly advance the date for the payment of the bill accordingly.

Thanking you

Yours faithfully

Shahid Latif

Ms. Celia
232, Hakikat Avenue
Quezon City

September 12, ...

To

The Deputy Commissioner
Queen City

Sir

I am a resident of Hakikat Nagar colony of this city. I wish to draw your attention to the deplorable condition of this colony. The colony was intended to be a model colony of the city. However, now it is one of the worst in the city. In the absence of proper civic amenities and because of the apathy of the concerned officers, the city is fast turning into a slum.

The roads in the colony are in a bad shape. Potholes on these roads make driving hazardous. In rainy season, these potholes are filled with water and prove dangerous traps for children. There are piles of rubbish and garbage lying here and there. The drains are not cleaned regularly and these have become breeding places for flies and mosquitoes. It is feared that an epidemic may break out here any moment.

I request you to pay a visit to the locality and see the things for yourselves. Please instruct the sanitary staff to clean the roads and drains regularly. Rubbish should also be removed from the roadsides daily.

Thanking you

Yours sincerely

Ms. Celia

R.M. Raina
348 Sarabha Nagar
Ludhiana

April 19, ...

To

The Superintending Engineer
Punjab State Electricity Board
Ludhiana.

Sir

I, on behalf of the residents of Sarabha Nagar, Ludhiana, wish to draw your attention to the electricity problems which we have been facing for about a week now. The power supply to this colony is highly erratic. The power supply remains cut off for long periods. As summer has set in, the power cuts make life miserable in the hot season. These are the examination days and the worse hit by these cuts are the school and college students whose studies have been adversely affected by the irregular power supply.

Apart from power cuts, there is great fluctuation in the voltage. The extreme fluctuations in voltage have resulted in damage to our costly electric and electronic gadgets. Sometimes the light is so dim that it is difficult to read in that light.

You are requested kindly to look into the matter and ensure continuous power supply without fluctuations.

Thanking you

Yours sincerely

R.M. Raina

Office of the Superintending Engineer
Punjab State Elec. Board
Ludhiana

April 18, ...

To

R.K. Raina
348 Sarabha Nagar
Ludhiana

Dear Mr. Raina

I am in receipt of your letter. I am sorry that you and other residents
of your colony have been facing difficulties due to power cuts and
inadequate power supply. The problem has arisen due to a defect in
one section of the power station No. II which feeds Sarabha Nagar
and the adjoining areas. We have been giving you power from the
other power station and hence we have to resort to load shedding and
power cuts as there is already a great load on that power house.

The repair work on power house No. II is being done on war footing
and is expected to be over in three-to four days after which the power
supply is likely to become normal once again. In the mean time,
kindly bear with us.

Thanking you

Yours Sincerely

R.K. Jain
Superintending Engineer

Ms. Carrol
974 Shiv Colony
Metro Manila

May 25, ...

To

The Medical Officer
Public Health Department
Metro Manila

**Sub : Adulterated and unhygienic food being served at
the Roxsons Restaurant, Metro Manila**

Sir

I wish to bring to your kind notice, that the food being served at the Roxons Restaurant which is one the post popular hotels in the town is adulterated and inhyiegnic.

On the 22nd of this month I visited the restaurant along with three of my guests in order to take dinner there. As we started eating, we found that the food was not upto the mark. A bad smell was coming from the chicken served by the restaurant. Perhaps the stale chicken had been served after heating it.

The flour used for making chapattis was also of the poor quality. We complained to the manager about it but he did not pay any heed to our complaint. On the other hand, he insisted on our making payment for the food that had been served to us. To avoid creating a scene, we paid for the food but came out without eating it.

You are requested to kindly make an on the spot inspection of the food and the hygienic standards at the Roxons Restaurant so that the management of the hotel does not play with the health of the public.

Thanking you,

Yours faithfully

Ms. Carrol

P.R. Khan
1088/5 Urban Estate
Sukkar

August 26, ...

M/s Durga Electronics
G.T. Road
Sukkur

Dear Sirs

On the first of this month, I purchased an Onida colour television (51 cm, model 44 YS) from your shop vide cash memo No. 4097. The set worked properly only for a week and since then it has been giving us trouble. The reception is poor. Beside blurring on the screen, there has been a constant jitter. The picture is not steady and keeps shaking. Some times for a few seconds, there is a complete black out. The brightness of the screen also keeps fluctuating. The sound is also not good and there is a constant noise. The sound level automatically keeps fluctuating.

The TV carries a two-year warrantee. So kindly send your mechanic immediately to look into the fault. It would be better if you replace the set with a new one.

Thanking you

Yours faithfully

P.R. Khan

Bishwajeet
23 Naraina Vihar
Annamalai Nagar
Chittagong

November 18, ...

The Chief Superintendent (Catering)
Railways
Rail Bhavan
Dhaka

Sir

I wish to bring to your notice the poor quality of food served on The Super Express. I was one of the passengers who travelled by the Super Express on November 16, ... from Dhaka to Chittagong. The lunch was served to us when the train was nearing the Docklane Junction.

The quality of the food was substandard. It did not match the other facilities available on the train. The food seemed to be adulterated as after 15 minutes of consuming the food, most of the passengers complained of uneasiness. Some of them vomited and some of the passengers were taken off the train at the next station and were admitted to the civil hospital for treatment.

It is apparent that the food was not checked thoroughly by your catering staff. I often find that utensils and pots are not properly cleaned. This is a grave negligence on the part of the concerned officials.

I request you to initiate an enquiry in this matter.

Thanking you and with kind regards,

Your faithfully

Bishwajeet

Subodh Shrivastava
129, Talkatora Lane
New Delhi

March 27, ...

The Controller of Examinations
Central Board of School Education
New Delhi.

Re : Request for re-evaluation of Class XII
Economics Paper

Sir,

I wish to bring to your kind notice that there seems to be some discrepancy in the marking of my paper of Economics I Class XII, the result of which was declared yesterday. The result shows that I have obtained 37 marks in this paper, which is barely pass mark.

Here I want to state that this mark in my Economics paper is contrary to· all logic and possibilities. I am counted among the intelligent students of the class and have always secured more than 75 per cent marks in this subject in all my school examinations. Secondly after appearing in the examination, I had discussed the Economics paper with my teacher and he calculated that I would get more than 80 per cent marks. What is more mysterious is that the student who never scored more than 40 percent marks has got 79 marks in this paper.

I suspect that there is either unfair marking or some other grave discrepancy in the declaration of result. I therefore, request you to kindly make a thorough investigation into the matter and get my Economics Paper re-evaluated.

Thanking you,

Yours faithfully

(Subodh Shrivastava)
Roll No. 79884, Class XII

Dated : 24th June, ...

From

The Controller of Examinations
Central Board of School Examination
New Delhi.

To

Shri Subodh Shrivastava
129, Talkatora Lane
New Delhi

Dear Shri Shrivastava

Re : Your letter dated .... for re-evaluation

I have received your complaint about the wrong marking of Economics Paper in XII class. I have directed the concerned official of my office to get your paper of Economics re-evaluated by a group of experienced teachers. I hope that they will do the needful within fifteen days after which your results of this class will be declared.

Thanking you,

Yours faithfully

(Subodh Shrivastava)

S.B. Koirala
184, Kuresong Colony
Kathmandu (Nepal)

October 24, ...

The Chief Executive Officer
Sanitation and Water supply division
Kathmandu

Sir,

Re : Erratic and inadequate water supply

I, on behalf of the residents of this colony, wish to bring to your kind notice the inadequate and erratic position of water supply in this area. Our colony is suffering from a grave water shortage crisis. Often either there is no water supply in the morning or the water pressure is so low just a thin trickle of water comes out of the taps which is not sufficient to meet the daily requirements. Most of the residents of this colony are employees and they do not have even a bucket of water to wash themselves before going to work.

Apart from the poor supply, the quality of the drinking water is also pitiable. Most of the time the water coming out of the taps is brackish and unhygienic. On one occasion, some residents complained of having found worms in the drinking water.

You are requested kindly to look the matter urgently and take immediate steps to remove our difficulties.

Thanking you,

Yours faithfully

S.B. Koirala

October 26, ...

From

    A.N. Bisht
    The Chief Executive Officer
    Sanitation and Water Supply division
    Kathmandu

To

    S.B. Koirala
    184, Kuresong Colony
    Kathmandu (Nepal)

      Sub : Your complaint about water shortage

Dear Mr. Koirala

Kindly refer to your letter of 24th October on the subject cited above.

In this connection, I wish to inform you that the main water pipe line carrying water to your colony had been damaged and the work was in progress to repair it. As a result we had to suspend the water supply to your colony for one day and thereafter partial water was temporarily diverted to your colony from other pipes as a result of which the water supply was at a lower pressure than usual. The pipe line has been repaired today and we are restoring the normal water supply to your area with immediate effect.

As regards your complaint about the quality of drinking water, I have immediately ordered Sh. Ranny Denzogpa, the Junior Public Health Engineer to look into the matter and take remedial measures at once.

Thanking you,

Yours sincerely

(A.N. Bisht)

Margaret Smith
76 Dock Lane
Mainway
Hongkong
August 20, ...

The Director
Delhi Tourism Corporation
21 B.K.S. Road
New Delhi

Sir,

International tourists are a good means of spreading goodwill among nations. After his brief visit to a country, an international tourist becomes a sort of cultural ambassador of that country as he tells his friends and relatives about the country he has visited. And if the tourist has had unsavoury experience in that country, he will create unpleasant and undesirable impression in the minds of others.

Unfortunately, I happen to be in the latter category. During my recent visit to your great country I had a number of pleasant and unpleasant experience. India has undoubtedly a great cultural heritage. Her monuments and the richness of culture left me spellbound. However, the behaviour of some people in India cast a black shadow on the otherwise pleasant experience.

I wish to bring to your kind notice the fleecing of tourists being done in your country by some unscruplous persons. The taxi and auto drivers fleece foreign tourists wherever they can. On one occasion , I was charged Rs. 200/- for which, I should have been charged not more than Rs. 70/-. Some tourist guides undertook to show me some monuments and found that they were as ignorant about the history of those monuments as myself.

The shopkeepers who sell different kinds of things outside the historical or religious monuments also cheat the tourists. They would hope to sell a thing of Rs. 50 for Rs. 500. The general impression among the tourist agents, hotel agents, taxi drivers and shopkeepers is that all foreign tourists are very rich and that they can be fleeced with impunity.

I would, therefore, request you to take stringent measures against those who fleece tourists and bring bad name to your country.

Thanking you,

Yours sincerely

(Margaret Smith)

DELHI TOURISM CORPORATION

21 B.K.S. Road
New Delhi

August 30, ...

Margaret Smith
76 Dock Lane
Mainway
Hongkong

Madam

Thanks for your letter of 20th August.

At the outset, I am extremely sorry that you have had some unpleasant experience during your visit to India a few weeks ago. I, on behalf of my countrymen, apologise for the inconvenience caused to you.

Madam, while I agree that a few unscruplous persons may bring bad name to a country. At the same time, I believe that generalisations are bad and you cannot give a label to the whole country or people on the basis of your experience with a few people. Let me assure you that we Indians are very cooperative and hold the visiting tourists in great respect. It is unfortunate that you had your contact with such persons as did not care for their country's image and left a bad impression upon you.

Upon receiving your letter I convened a meeting of my colleagues and decided upon the steps to be taken to prevent the possible repetition of the kind of experience you had in India. I assure you that we are soon taking steps to prevent the fleecing of tourists by the taxi drivers, hotel and tourists guides.

Thanking you

Yours Sincerely

(R.K. Soni)
Director

P. D'Souza
92 Christian Colony
Colombo

August 29, ...

The Postmaster
General Post Office
Colombo

Dear Sir

I wish to bring to your notice the late delivery of mail in our area. Mr. Vijita, the postman of this beat, is very negligent in his duties. He never delivers the mail on time. Today he delivered the letter which carried the local postal stamp of 16th August. Even registered letters are delivered late.

The delivery of mail is not only late, it is irregular also. Sometimes, he does not visit his beat and delivers the letters of that day early next morning.

Sometimes, the postman throws letters just outside the gate and often he delivers our letters to wrong addresses in the colony. This is highly objectionable. You are requested to kindly take strict action against him so that he delivers the mail on time.

Thanking you

Yours faithfully

P. D'Souza

Ashok Mahapatra
340, Reddy Nagar
Yangoon

February 26, ...

The Superintendent of Police
Yangoon

Sir

Of late, there has been a perceptible fall in the law and order situation in the city. The number of thefts has considerably increased. It is no longer safe for a person to go out of the city leaving his house unguarded. In three cases there have been robberies when armed persons forcibly entered the house and decamped with valuables after severely injuring the members of the household. In one case, an elderly man who had been badly beaten, succumbed to his injuries two days later. These thefts have become so common that the residents of the city spend restless nights.

Apart from thefts, there have been a number of cases of murders, chain snatching and vandalism. Four cases of rape were reported from the city during the last year. As you are well aware, the abduction of Kahul Jabaj for ransom from out city caused a great sensation all over the country.

Thus, you will find that the law and order situation in our city is fast deteriorating. Therefore, I request you to take immediate steps to curb the crime and anti-social elements. The need of the hour is to increase the police patrolling throughout the city. The criminals who are apprehended should be severely dealt with.

I hope you will pay adequate attention to my request.

Thanking you

Yours faithfully

(Ashok Mahapatra)

X. APPLICATIONS FOR JOBS

93. Application for the post of a supervisor

Raymond Matthews
354, Rose Gardens
Bangkok (Thailand)

March 8, ...

The General Manager
Hyde Park Enterprises
764, Westend Block
Bangkok (Thailand)

Sir,

In response to your advertisement in the Bangkok Post today, I offer myself as one of the candidates for the post of a supervisor in your concern.

I graduated from the University of Bangkok with a high second class. After that I obtained a diploma in garment manufacturing from the Japanese Institute of Garment Manufacturing Technology, Tokyo.

I have been working as a Supervisor of production Unit in a garment factory at Angkor for the last two years. But the conditions of work here are not good. At the same time, the emoluments are not very encouraging. Hence, I wish to switch over to a better and more reputed company. It is with this aim in mind that I seek this job in your concern.

I am 26 years old and possess a pleasing personality and amiable manners.

In case I get an opportunity to join your esteemed concern, I shall leave no stone unturned to prove myself worthy of my selection.

Thanking you in anticipation,

Yours faithfully

Raymond Matthews

Robert Wadheira
654, Civil Lones
Hyderabad

May 16, ...

The Director
All India Radio
Hyderabad Radio Station
Hyderabad

Dear Sir

In response to your advertisement in the Times of India of today, for the post of announcers for All India Radio, Hyderabad, I offer myself as one of the candidates for the said post.

My qualifications and experience are as under :

I am a graduate from the Osmania University, Hyderabad, with a high second division.

I have a pleasing voice. I have passed the audition test conducted by the All India Radio, New Delhi.

During my college career, I took keen interest in singing and drama. I was a member of my college drama team. I won a number of prizes because of my talent for acting.

I took keen interest in speeches and declamation contests and won a number of prizes in them.

I am a good singer also and have participated as a singer in four annual Youth Festivals during my stay in the college.

I took part in a debate on the evil of drinking which was broadcast from the Delhi station of All India Radio.

I have a high I.Q. and take a keen interest in Indian history, culture and current events.

If given a chance to be an announcer, I will not only satisfy you with my work but will also be a great favourite with the listeners of your programmes.

I hope that you will kindly give me a chance to serve the All India Radio, Hyderabad.

Thanking you

Yours faithfully

Robert Wadheira

Enclosed : Testimonials

Safeena Click
14 Bradford Road
London

July 18, ...

The Managing Director
Discovery Communications Pvt Ltd
14 Picadily
London

Dear Sir

I came across, in yesterday's Times, your advertisement regarding your need for a Director for your fothcoming TV serial.

In this connection, I wish to offer my services to direct the above serial. I give below my qualifications in brief.

I passed my M.A. from the Pune University in 19 ...... and then I obtained a diploma in Film Direction from the Indian Film Institute, Pune.

I am a man of 45 years with a perfect health and a zeal for work. I possess enough stamina to cope with the multifarious jobs a direction of TV serials has to perform.

Perhaps you are familiar with my name as I have directed the first thirty episodes of the mega serial "Children's Love". But then due to certain circustances, I had to quit the team of that serial.

I directed the highly successful serial "Lovers Paradise" in which selina made her debut.

Then I was associated with Mr. Geofry as assistant director and directed several episodes of the great serial 'Budha'. I have directed a few tele-plays also.

The serials or episodes directed by me have been highly praised by the viewers and critics.

I assure you that if I am given chance to direct your forthcoming serial, it will be a great success and will top the chart of popularity.

Hoping to hear from you soon.

Yours sincerely

Safeena Click

Mushir Ahmed
954, Bani Park
Lahore

16 April, ...

The President
Hamdard Trust
Lahore

Sir

With reference to your advertisement in the Pakistan Times of today, I hereby apply for the post of Principal in your college. My academic and administrative experience is as under :

1. I passed my M.A. in Economics from the Lahore University in 19 ......, securing a high first class.

2. Then I passed my M.Phil (Economics) examination from the same university and won a gold medal.

3. Thereafter, I joined the Karachi University as a research scholar, doing my Ph.D. in Economics. The topic of my research was : An economic survey of the Biharis of the Sind Area.

4. I joined St. Stephens College, Islamabad as a lecturer in Economics and served that institution for seven years.

5. Then I was selected Vice-Principal of Commerce College. I have been holding that post for the last five years.

6. As a Vice-Principal, I streamlined the working of the college. I have maintained a good rapport both with the students and the teachers. The result of my college have been excellent. Many students of our college won scholarships and secured merit positions.

7. I am a good writer also. My books on Economics are widely read all over Pakistan. These books have been acclaimed by students.

8. Our college has a reputation in the field of cultural activities and sports. Some of our sportsmen have won national honours.

At present I am 48 years of age, but I possess a sound health and stamina to perform the duties of a principal.

I hope that you will be kind enough to consider my application favourably.

Thanking you

Yours faithfully

Mushir Ahmed

Bath Ocampo
D'Silva Line
Manila

July 23, ...

Personnel Manager
M/s Vikas Publishers
Swindon Road
Manila

Dear Sir

I have come to know from a reliabale source that you require the services of a cashier. So, I take the liberty of submitting my usolicited application for the same post.

I am a first class Commerce graduate from Manila University. After that I worked as a cashier with a local firm. In that firm I prepared the pay rolls of the employees. Then my father was transferred to Hongkong and my family was shifted here. As the salary offered by that firm was not much it was not an attractive propostion to live there alone. So I had to resign the job.

I am a young girl of 25 years having a good health and excellent character. Moreover, I know type-writing and have knowledge of computers also. I know how to use computer for the efficient and quick discharge of the office work.

Regarding my salary, I am prepared to accept any suitable amount which you consider proper keeping in view my qualifications and experience.

Sir, I wish to assure you that if I am selected, I will discharge my duties efficiently and to your entire satisfaction.

I hope you will give me a chance to serve you.

Thank you

Yours faithfully

Beth Ocampo

Remo Fernandes
29, Parliament Street
Tehran

October 19, ...

The Managing Director
State Paints and Varnishes Ltd
Tehran

Dear Sir,

This is with reference to your advertisement in the Khaleej Times for the post of an Office Assistant in your organisation. In this connection, I request you to consider my candidature for the same.

I am a young man of 25 years and possess an excellent health. I am a very hard working man and have the ability to take up challenging jobs.

I have an excellent educational career. I was placed at No. 2 in the merit list of XII class in my senior secondary examination. I passed my graduation in First Division with distinction in English. After that I learnt typewriting and my speed is 60 words per minutes. Apart from this, I have a good knowledge of using computers for the office work.

I worked for two years as a clerk in a private firm that manufactures clothes. I am conversant with the accounts work and office procedure.

I request you to consider my candidature for the above job favourably keeping in view my qualifications and experience.

Thanking you

Yours faithfully

Remo Fernandes

Remo Fernandes
29, Parliament Street
Tehran

May 26, ...

The Managing Director
State Paints and Varnishes Ltd.
Tehran

Dear Sir

This is with reference to your advertisement in The Tehran Times for the post of an Office Assistant. I request you to consider my candidature for the same.

I am giving below a brief biodata of mine, which gives the particulars of my qualifications, experience, general aptitude and other pertinent details :

1.	Name	Remo Fernandes
2.	Age and health	25 years with a sound health and an excellent personality
3.	Address :	29, Parliament Street, Tehran
4.	Academic Qualifications :	(a) Senior Secondary in Ist class. (b) B.A. in first division with distinction.
5.	Experience :	(a) Worked with Duke and Co. Tehran, for two years.
6.	General aptitude :	(a) Accounts maintenance (b) Knowledge of computers (c) General office procedure (d) Typing : 60 words per minutes
7.	Special Achievements :	(a) Won a number of academic prizes during college time. (b) Won many prizes in sports and debates.
8.	Salary acceptable :	As per company's rules.

I hope you will give me an opportunity to serve your organisation.
I am enclosing copies of my educational and experience certificates.

Thank you

Yours faithfully

Remo Fernandes

Shiv Raj Patil
765, Visakha Nagar
Pitampura,
New Delhi.

March 20, ...

M/s Madras Refineries Pvt Ltd.
36 T. Nagar
Chennai (Tamil Nadu)

Dear Sirs

Re : Post of a Labour Welfare Officer

This is with reference to your recent advertisement in the Indian Express for the post of a Labour Welfare Officer in your concern. I hereby apply for the same. My qualifications and experience, are as under :

(a) I passed my B.A. examination from the Annamali University with a first division.

(b) Thereafter I obtained a Diploma in Labour Welfarre from the same University.

(c) I passed my LLB examination with specialisation in labour laws from the Delhi University.

(d) After completing my education, I joined M/s Global Sea Foods Limited as an Astt. Labour Welfare Officer and have been in that service for five years. My employers are fully satisfied with my work and conduct. Here, I have been instrumental in solving a number of problems between the labour and the management. I am popular both with the management and the workers.

(e) I possess tact and shrewdness, the qualities which are necessary in a labour welfare officer.

(f) I am interested in labour welfare. At the same time, I believe that there must be a proper balance between management and the workers. If the management should take care of the needs of the labour class, the workers should also safeguard the inteests of the management.

(g) I am a young man of 27 years with a sound physique and good moral character.

I hope you will consider my application favourably.

Thanking you

Yours faithfully

Shiv Raj Patil

Pratik Kumar
62, Suryalok Building
(2nd Floor), Rajendra Nagar
New Delhi

September 20, ...

The Under Secretary
Minister of Sports
South Block
New Delhi

Dear Sir,

Reg : Post of Section Officer (Accounts)

With reference to your advertisement in the Hindustan Times of 10th September, for the post of a Section Officer (Accounts), I take this opportunity to offer my services for the same.

The details regarding my educational qualifications and experience are furnished below.

A. QUALIFICATIONS

(a) I passed my B.Com examination with honours in Accountancy from the Indore University in 19 ......

(b) I got a scholarship for higher studies and obtained a diploma in accountancy from Narsee Monjee College of Commerce, Mumbai.

(c) I have an excellent academic career throughout. I topped the state list in my Senior Secondary Examination.

(d) I have a diploma in Chartered Accountancy which I obtained from the Indian Institute of Chartered Accountants.

B. EXPERIENCE

I joined M/s Wadhera Textile Mills as a cashier in 19 ...... and served that concern for two years.

Thereafter I left the job as M/s Nicholson Steel Mills offered me the job of an accountant which was better paid. I have been in this job for the last four years.

I have gained enough experience in all aspects of accountancy, for example, preparing of accounts, salary bill accounts, budget, balance sheets, etc.

C. AGE AND RELATED PARTICULARS

I am a young man of 30 years and possess a sound physique and a good moral character. I am a hard working man and am capable of working for long hours after the office time if there is need.

D. OTHER PARTICULARS.

(a) I know typing and my speed is 50 words per minute.

(b) I know how to run computers. I am well versed in accounting software on the computer.

In the end, I assure that if I am selected, I will prove worthy of this job.

Thank you

Yours faithfully

(Pratik Kumar)

Rafiq Ahmed
17, Ibraham Road
Quetta

June 25, ...

The Managing Director
Ferguson Engineering Works
9, Lake Road, Sukkur

Dear Sir

In response to your advertisement in the Dawn of 20th June, for the post of Purchase Manager, I hereby apply for the same.

A brief resume of my qualifications and experience is given below :

Qualifications : (a) B.A. with a first class from the Baluchistan University in 19......

(b) M. Com. with a good second division from Islamabad University.

Experience : (a) Worked as purchase assistant in Avon Industries Multan for three years.

(b) Thereafter I joined M/s Atlas Cycle Co, Bahawalpur as Asst. Purchase Manager and have been holding that position for the last 4 years.

During this period, I acquired experience of labour procurement for the factory. This experience of mine will go a long way if I am given a job in your concern.

Age : 28 years of age with good health.

Salary expected : Rs. 18,000 per month plus perks.

I hope that keeping in view my qualifications and experience, you will give me a chance to serve your concern as a Purchase Manager.

Thank you,

Yours faithfully

Rafiq Ahmed

Benjamin Gilani
981, Larkin Road
Dublin

August 20, ...

Messers Unique Publishers
119, Ibrahim Avenue
Dublin

Dear Sirs

From your recent advertisement in Dublin Times, I came to know that you need a general clerk for your publishing concern. As my general qualifications and capabilities quite match the requirements for this post, I offer my services for it.

I passed my B.A. in 19.... obtaining 76% marks. After that I acquired diploma in Secretarial Practice and have acquired general proficiency in office routine activities.

I am a young man of 25 years and possess a sound physique and an excellent moral character. I can travel extensively on official work and can work in any of your branches in other cities.

My handwriting is very good and I know typing as well. My speed in typewriting is 60 words per minute. I have a basic and working knowledge of computers also which will greatly help me in the discharge of my duties.

At present I am working on part time basis with M/s Sonia Books, Dublin. This job has given me experience in the book trade. I know how to prepare invoices, approach libraries for books supply, how to deal with the paper suppliers, etc. Therefore, I feel myself suitable for the post of a general clerk in your concern.

I am prepared to accept the job at the starting scale of general clerk in your concern.

I am enclosing herewith attested copies of my B.A. certificate and other testimonials which will tell you about my accomplishment and suitability for this job.

I assure you that if given a chance to serve you, I'll prove to be an asset to your concern. I hope you will consider my application favourably.

Thank you

Yours faithfully

Benjamin Gilani

Rohin Singh
146 Parliament Road
Baghdad

April 27, ...

The Personnel Manager
Bill Gates Computers Ltd.
145, MG Road
Baghdad

Subject : Application for the post of Office Superintendent

Dear Sir

I request you to consider my candidature for the post of Office superintendent in your concern, an advertisement for which appeared in the Times of India of 20th April.

I am a young man of 25 years. I shall be twenty six in December.

I did my graduation and M.A. in Economics. Thereafter, I joined M/s Ambani Textiles as a general office assistant. After three years I was promoted as office superintendent, the position which I still occupy. Due to certain matters concerning my promotion, I wish to leave this concern and find a better firm to work with. So I offer my services to you.

At present I am getting a salary of $2,000 per month. If selected, I would like to get $3,000 per month.

I am enclosing herewith my service certificate which speaks of my good record and efficient working. Attested copies of my certificates and testimonials are also enclosed.

I hope you will give me a chance to serve you.

Thank you

Yours faithfully

Robin Singh

Kamal Hasan
642, Maurya Enclave
Ipoh Road
Penang

May 15, ...

M/s Amir Khan & Co.
311, Jalan Usman
Penang

Dear Sirs

With reference to your advertisement in the Strait Times, for the post of a Travelling Salesman. In response to that I hereby submit my application for the same.

My qualifications and experience in this field are given below :

(a) I am a young man of 25 years with an excellent health.

(b) I passed my B.A. examination four years ago from University of malaya, Kuala Lumpur with a first class.

(c) For the last three years, I have been working with M/s Swiss Watch Co., and possess enough experience in this line.

(d) I have a pleasing personality and possess the art of presuading others.

(e) With my tact and experience, I can bring a lot of business to your concern.

Sir, to begin with, you can keep me on probation for six months, and if you are satisfied with my ability, you can then absorb me in your organisation on permanent basis.

Hoping to receive a reply from you soon,

Yours faithfully

Kamal Hasan

Rajiv Kumar
Z-2, West Patel Nagar
New Delhi

June 20, ...

The Managing Director
Hindustan Textile Mills Ltd.
Mumbai

Dear Sir

Re : Post of a Works Manager

Apropos to your advertisement in the Financial Times of 20th February for the post of a works manager, I request you to consider me as one of the candidates.

I furnish below details of my qualifications and experience. A perusal of these particulars will convince you that I am an ideal choice for this post.

(a) I got a diploma in mechanical engineering from IIT, Delhi in 19 ...... and started my own business.

(b) Due to certain unforeseen circumstances, I had to wind up my business. I then joined M/s Tirupati Industries as a foreman. I have been holding that position for the 1st five years.

(c) I have gained wide-ranging experience regarding the working of textile mills and will be highly helpful to you as a works manager.

I am a young man of 28 years with a good health and a pleasing personality. I am a hard working man and have a knack for taking up challenging jobs.

I assure you that if given a chance to join your business house, I will prove myself worthy of the trust reposed in me. I will be able to satisfy you with my work and conduct.

The matter of salary can be discussed at the time of interview.

I hope that you will give me a chance to be associated with your prestigious concern.

Thanking you

Yours faithfully

Rajiv Kumar

Sadhna Pandey
B-75, Teachers' Colony
Allahabad
10th May, ...

M/s Kolynos Products
16, Hospital Road
New Delhi

Dear Sirs,

This has a reference to your advertisement in The Indian Express of Ist May, for the post of a Telephone Operator cum-Receptionist in your concern. I request you to consider me for this job.

I have a good academic record. I passed my senior secondary examination with 80 per cent marks and was placed at number four in the merit list of the CBSE examination. I graduated from Allahabad University, Allahabad last year in the first division. After that I did diploma in secretarial practice as well as learnt the use of computers. I am fluent in English, Hindi and Punjabi.

After obtaining my bachelor's degree, I worked as a telephone operator with M/s Vardhman Spinning mills. As the post was temporary, I had to leave it. Then I joined M/s Sham Lal and Sons as a telephone operator cum receptionist where I am still continuing. But as the conditions here are not condusive to work. I am in search of a better organisation to work with. As your company enjoys a better reputation, I wish to join it.

I am a young woman of 25 years with a pleasing personality and attractive manners. I am enclosing herewith copies of testimonials from my previous and present employers. A passport size photograph of mine is also enclosed.

At present, I am drawing a salary of Rs. 5000 per month, and if selected, I would like to get a higher start. However, the matter can be negotiated at the time of interview.

Thanking you

Yours faithfully

Sadhna Pandey

Ishfaq Hussain
Janab-ul Hasan Road
Abu Dhabi

April 12, ...

The General Manager
KYL Wire Company
Rashid Mohammed Road
Abu Dhabi (UAE)

Dear Sir

This has a reference to your advertisement published in the Khaleeg Times of today regarding your need to recruit a Foreman (furnace). I take this opportunity to offer myself as a candidate of this post.

As regards my qualifications I wish to state that I did my B.Sc. with Physics in 19...... Thereafter, I obtained a diploma in Steel-Wire technology.

At present I have been working as a Foreman with M/s Sirmor Steel Wires & Co. for the last two years. My employers are fully satisfied with my work. here I am engaged in the work of coating of steel wires and I am fully conversant with the latest techniques involved in this job.

I am a young man of 23 years having a robust health and a good moral character.

I hope you will be kind enough to grant me this opportunity to serve you. In that case I will do my utmost to satisfy you with my work and conduct.

I am enclosing herewith copies of my certificates and testimonials for your ready reference.

Thanking you in anticipation,

Yours faithfully

Ishfaq Hussain

Encl. : Attested copies of certificates.

Ishfaq Hussain
Janab-ul Hasan Road
Abu Dhabi (UAE)

May 13, ...

The General Manager
HYL Wire Company
Rashid Mohammed Road
Abu Dhabi (UAE)

Dear Sir

With reference to your advertisement published in the Khaleeg Times today, for the post of a Foreman, I hereby offer my services for the same post.

As regards my qualifications I wish to point out that I am a first class B.Sc. with Physics as the major subject. I got a merit position in the University. After that I obtained a diploma in Steel Wire Industry.

Sir, although I have no experience of working as a foreman (furnace). Yet I feel myself suitable for this job. I have been reading enough material on the steel-wire coating and heat-treatment technology. I have visited some steel wire factories and watched personally the technique employed in this process. I have learnt practically all these techniques.

I am a young man of 24 years with robust health and a determination to meet challenging tasks.

I assure you Sir, that my lack of experience will not come in the way of the smooth discharge of my duties. Moreover, Sir, we must not forget that even a long journey begins with a single step. Nobody can gain experience unless someone is prepared to give him a chance to prove his worth.

I hope that I will given a chance to serve you.

Thanking you,

Yours faithfully

Ishfaq Hussain

Mohan Rakesh
22, Vivekananda Nagar
Ambala (Haryana)

March 8 ......

The Managing Director
Creative Advertisers
Baba Kharak Singh Marg
New Delhi- 110001

Sir

Please refer to your advertisement for the post of a Media Assistant in your Advertising concern. I take this opportunity to apply for the same.

As regards my qualifications and experience, I have to state as under :

I passed my B.A. Examination from Kurukshetra University in 19 ...... Thereafter I obtained a diploma in journalism and Public Relations.

I am also a diploma holder in Art which I obtained from the Indian Institute pf Fine Arts, New Delhi.

During my studies, I took keen interest in extra-curricular activities. I took part in debates, singing and painting.

I have great organisational skill. I can organise functions, sale campaigns, or advertising campaigns sucessfully.

I have been working as a Media Assistant in the Sunshine Advertising Agency, New Delhi, for the last four years. I have satisfied my employers with my work and aptitude. But because the promotion avenues in this company are almost nil, I wish to join a more reputed company like yours where there is scope for the expression of my creative abilities.

I am a young man of 27 years, having good health, a pleasing personality and amiable manners.

I hope you will give a chance to serve you.

Thanking you

Yours faithfully

Mohan Rakesh

Rosy Moody
Farrington Street
Djakarta

June 15, ...

The General Manager
Roussel India Ltd.
6, Coronation Point
Djakarta

Sir

Kindly refer to your advertisement in The Djakarta Times of today. In this connection, I offer myself as one of the candidates for the post of Supervisor in your concern.

I graduated from the Indonesia University with a high second class. After that I obtained a diploma in garment manufacturing from the Manila Institute of Garment Manufacturing Technology, Djakarta.

I have been working as a Supervisor of production unit in a garment factory at Djakarta for the last 2 years. But the conditions of work here are not congenial. At the same time, The emoluments are not very encouraging. Hence I wish to switch over to a better and more reputed company. It is with this thing in mind that I seek this job in your concern.

I am 26 years and possess a pleasing personality and amiable manners.

In case I get an opportunity to join your esteemed concern. I will leave no stone unturned to prove myself worthy of my selection.

Thanking you in anticipation,

Yours faithfully

Rosy Moody

A. K. Baweja
34, Soni Enclave
Meerut (U.P.)

July 10, ...

The Managing Director
Oberoi Intercontinental
New Delhi

Dear Sir

Re. : Post of a Manager

This is with reference to your advertisement in the Hindustan Times, New Delhi regarding filling up the post of a Manager at your Five Star Hotel. In this connection, I request you to consider me as one of the candidates.

Details regarding my qualifications and experience are given below :

I am a young man of twenty eight years with good health, a pleasing personality and amiable manners.

After completing my graduation from the Lucknow University with first class, I obtained a diploma in Hotel Management from the Northern Indian Institute of Hotel Management and Catering, Sonepat (Haryana).

Thereafter, I joined the Mahak Restaurant in Chandigarh as a Steward and worked there for two years. The management of the restaurant was very pleased with my amiable behaviour with the customers.

Then I got an offer for a higher opening at Hotel Kapil in Chandigarh. Here I have been working as an Assistant Manager. My job includes looking after the customers, the waiting staff and the kitchen staff.

But it is only a three star hotel and there are very few avenues for promotion. Therefore, I wish to be associated with a reputed Hotel like yours.

I assure you, Sir, that if I get a chance to serve your hotel, I will look after all the aspects of the running a modern five star hotel. If selected, I would like to get a salary of about six thousand rupees per month.

Thanking you in anticipation,

Yours faithfully

A.K. Baweja

S. John
23/Z Star Enclave
New Delhi

The Director
Jaslok Hospital
Bombay

Re. : Post of a Dental Surgeon

Dear Sir

Kindly refer to your advertisement in the Hindustan Times of today regarding the vacancy of a Dental Surgeon in your hospital. As I consider myself a suitable candidate for this job, I take this opportunity to apply for the same.

I furnish below my qualification and experience for your kind perusal.

1. I passed my B.D.S. examination from King George Medical College and Hospital, Lucknow (affiliated with the Lucknow University) in 19......

2. Then I got scholarship from the Govt. of India and attended a six-month advance refresher course in modern dentistry at Montreal (Canada).

3. On my return to India I joined a temporary post as Asst. Dental Surgeon in Government Clinic in a small village of Rajasthan. But as the post was against a leave vacancy, I was relieved of my duties when the permanent incumbent of the post returned from leave.

4. Thereafter I joined the Jesus and Mary Dental Surgeon. I have been in this post for the last two years. During this time, I have gained valuable experience about all aspects of dentistry,

I have gained knowledge of the latest techniques about proper dental care.

Thus I have rich and varied experience of my job and therefore, hope that you will consider my application favourably.

Thanking you

Yours faithfully

S. John

Ahmed Bhatt
23, MI Road
Riyadh

June 18, ...

The Chief Editor
The Times of Riyadh
Bahadur Shah Zafar Road
Riyadh

Re : Post of a Journalist

Sir

In response to your advertisement in the Times of Riyadh of yesterday, I take this opportunity to apply for the post of a Journalist in your paper.

The particulars of my qualifications and experience are given below :

1. I did my M.A. in English in 19.......

2. Then I obtained a diploma in journalism from the Dubai Institute of Mass Communications, Dubai.

3. After completing my studies, I joined The Tribune as a reporter for Bahraen and the adjoining regions. I did my work deligently for seven years. During this period, I was always first with the news of that area. On many occasions, I dug out news before other reporters could even get the scent of it.

4. Then I left this newspaper and joined the BBC as their Riyadh correspondent. I have been holding this position for the last three years. The BBC bosses have been quite satisfied with my performance. I have provided them with a number of major scoops which has enhanced their credibility in India.

5. I am highly experienced in investigative journalism and have dug out a number of scams.

6. I am skilled in collecting and writing news, preparing write-ups and articles. I have a flair for writing and my write-ups have been greatly liked by the reading public.

Sir, as your chain of newspapers is the biggest in India and the papers of your group enjoys a lot of reputation in India and abroad, it will be an honour to work for you. It is with this aim in view that I wish to leave the BBC and join your paper as a journalist.

I am a young man of 5 years with a tough body which can withstand the demands of this profession. I am capable of extensive travelling which this profession often requires.

I assure you that if I am selected for this job, I will prove to be an asset to your newspaper.

Thank you

Yours faithfully

(Ahmed Bhatt)

Ashok Malhotra
25, DMC, Colony
Shimla (H.P.).

September 25, ...

M/s Kainaat Apple Orchards Ltd.
12, Lake Area
Shrinagar (J & K)

Dear Sirs,.

Re. : Post of a Horticultural Officer

With reference to your advertisement published last week in The Tribune for the post of a Horticultural Officer for your apple orchard, I hereby offer my services for this job.

As regards my qualifications and experience I point out that in 19......
I passed my B.Sc. (Agri.) from the Haryana Agricultural University, Hisar with my major subject being Fruit Plants.

Two years later I passed my M.Sc. (Horticulture) from the Horticulture Department of the same University. In my M.Sc., I opted for a special paper on apples.

Then I joined the Andhra Pradesh Agricultural University, Rajender Nagar as a Lecturer in Horticulture. I remained in that post for two years. But as I intended to pursue higher studies, I resigned the job.

I joined the H.A.U., Hisar again, this time in the Ph.D. Course. My research supervisor for Ph.D. was the world renowned Geneticicst, Dr. S.N. Kakar. My topic for the Ph.D. was "Improvement in the quality of Indian Apples " The results of my findings have been lauded by agricultural scientist all over India.

I have written a number of research papers on horticulture, particularly on apples and their improvement. These papers have been acclaimed in India and abroad.

I am a young man of 30 years possessing an excellent health and a sound moral character.

I assure you that if I am given a chance to serve your concern, I will devote my whole time and energies to the evolving of a disease free and better qualities of apples at your orchard.

Yours faithfully

Ashok Malhotra

XI. INTERVIEW AND APPOINTMENT LETTERS, RESIGNATIONS AND DISMISSALS

116. An Interview Letter

MAHENDRA ENGINEERING WORKS

115, K.G. Road
Mumbai-400031

August 21, ...

Sh. H.S. Chawla
234 Triveni Sangam Marg
Allahabad (U.P.)

Dear Mr. Chawla

This is with reference to your application for the post of a mechanical engineer.

You are requested to appear for an interview for the said post on 1st September, 19...... at 10.30 a.m. in the office of the undersigned.

You will be paid first class railway fare (both ways) from your city to the Mumbai. For claiming the fare, you will have to produce the ticket or the railway money receipt.

Please bring with you your certificates and testimonials in original for verification.

Thanks,

Yours sincerely

for Mahendra Engg. Works
Manager

ALECT STEWART AND COMPANY LTD.

564, High Street
East End, London

March 19, ...

Mr. Mark Spenser
Fairy Queen Street
London

Dear Sir

This is with reference to your application for the post of a Stenographer in our concern.

We regret to inform you that on primary scrutiny of your application we do not find your qualifications and experience up to our expectations.

Hence, it is not possible to call you for an interview for the said post.

We, however, thank you for the interest shown by you in our concern.

Thanking you

Yours sincerely

Managing Director

BHARAT HEAVY ELECTRICALS LTD.

22, Garden Lake Road
New Delhi

April 28, ...

Mr. V.M. Chandana
87, Rose Garden Road
Chandigarh

Dear Mr. Chandana

Kindly refer to your application dated 24th April, for the post of Refrigeration Engineer in our concern and the subsequent interview for the same.

It gives me great pleasure to inform you that you have been selected for this post as per the following terms and conditions :

You have been appointed in the pay scale of Rs. 3500-150-5000-300-8000 plus usual allowances as per our company rules. Your starting salary comes to about Rs. 10,000/-.

You will be on probation for a period of six months. During this period, if the management does not find your work satisfactory, they have the right to dismiss you without any notice.

After the successful completion of the probationary period, you will be deemed to be one of the permanent employees of the company. Then the company can terminate your services only after giving a three months notice and assigning proper reasons. Similarly, if you wish to resign your job, you will have to give us a three months notice. If you don't give three months notice, you will have a deposit money equal to the salary for the period by which the notice falls short of three months.

You have to abide by the service rules framed by the Company. Any breach of these rules may invite disciplinary action or even dismissal from the job.

You will be required to work honestly and to the entire satisfaction of your officers.

You will have to fill up a service contract stating that you will not work against the interests of your employers.

Thanking you

Yours sincerely

General Manager

DEPARTMENT OF TELECOMMUNICATIONS
(Govt. of Sri Lanka)

23, D'Silva Road
Colombo

November 12, ...

Dr. Ashok Gehlot M.B.B.S.
Gehlot Clinic
65, Surya Enclave
Colombo

Dear Sir

Recently, we advertised for the post of a foreman in our concern. The candidates were asked to give the names of three references.

One of the candidates, Mr. M. Subramanyam has given your name as a reference.

You are requested kindly to testify as to his knowledge and capabilities. Kindly also let us know about the character, sincerity and moral conduct of Mr. M. Subramanyam.

Your information will be kept entirely confidential.

Thanking you,

Yours sincerely

For Sri Lanka Steels Ltd.
General Manager

Dr. Ashok Gehlot M.B.B.S.
Gehlot Clinic
65, Surya Enclave
Colombo

October 15 ....

M/s Sri Lanka Steels Ltd.
432, Airport Road
Colombo

Dear Sirs

Kindly refer to your letter dated 10th October, 19...... vide which you have asked me to furnish information about Mr. M. Subramanyam, one of the candidates for the post of Foreman in your concern.

In this connection, I wish to point out that I have known Mr. M. Subramanyam for the last six years. During this period, I have found him to be a hardworking and sincere person. He possesses a high IQ and has the ability to meet the challenging tasks. I am sure, if he is selected as Foreman. He will prove to be an asset to you.

Thanking you

Yours faithfully

(Dr.) Ashok Gehlot

June 15, ...

To

The Managing Director
Sindh Steel Plant
Karachi

Sir

I wish to bring to your kind notice that I got married last month. My husband is posted at Lahore. So it is very difficult for me to remain at Karachi. Moreover, he has arranged a job for me there.

Hence, I cannot continue with my present job in you concern. I am, Therefore, submitting my resignation with effect from June 18, 19...... which constitutes one month's notice, as per Rules stipulated in my appointment letter.

I also request you to relieve me as soon as the period of notice expires.

Thanking you

Yours faithfully

Ruksana Sultan
P.A. to M.D.

DEPARTMENT OF GENETICS
HARYANA AGRICULTURAL UNIVERSITY
HISSAR

July 18, ...

It gives me great pleasure to certify that Sh. Harcharan Singh Sodhi worked as a Technician in this concern for four years, *i.e.* from 7th March, 19...... to 6th March, 19....... .

During this period, I found that Sh. Sodhi worked diligently and with dedication. His honesty and amiable temperament won the heart of practically every one in this concern.

His complete involvement with the work assigned to him and his resourcefulness are two of his most remarkable traits. He satisfied his superiors with his work and conduct.

Mr. Sodhi has resigned from his job on account of his own sweet will.

I wish him all success in life.

S.N. Kakar
Head, Deptt. of Genetics

J.C. Pinto
58, Rock Garden Road
Geneva

April 12, ...

The General Manager
M/s Swiss Manufacturing Ltd.
55, Garden Lake Road
Chennai

Sir

Kindly refer to your letter dated 10th April......... I am thankful to you for selecting me for the above post.

However, I regret to inform you that it will not be possible for me to join you Institution. I have got only yesterday, appointment in another firm on a higher starting salary.

Thanking you,

Yours faithfully

J.C. Pinto

DIRECTORATE OF CULTURAL AFFAIRS

213, Barakhamba Road
Dhaka

July 15, ...

Mr. Mohd. Ayub
Assistant superintendent
Directoral of Cultural Affairs
Dhaka

Sub : Dismissal from the post of Asstt. Superintendent

It is to inform you that a meeting of the committee constituted to look into the charges of misappropriation of money and leaking of official information against you was held yesterday. The committee also considered your reply to the charge sheet served to you. The committee found your explanation completely unsatisfactory.

The committee also interviewed other employees of the directorate and from their investigation, your charge has been established beyond doubt. You were given a chance last year to improve yourself but you went on with your corrupt ways.

I am, therefore, constrained to dismiss you from the post of Asst. Superintendent with immediate effect. According to service conditions, your employer may either give you a one month notice to quit or may dismiss you with immediate effect giving you one month's salary. The committee has chosen the latter alternative. You may, therefore, collect one month's salary in addition to your wages due for the previous month.

Director

XII. LETTERS TO THE EDITOR

---

125. *About the pollution created by a smoke-emitting factory near a residential area*

Kim Yung Lee
981 Leforge Street
Sun Yat Square
Singapore

July 20, ...

The Editor
Singapore Times
Singapore

Sir

Through the columns of your esteemed newspaper, I wish to draw the attention of the authorities to the pollution created in our colony by Che Guevra Textile Mills. Sun Yat Square is a residential area and the residents are at a loss to understand why this factory has been allowed to come in close proximity to this colony. The presence of the Textile Mills is a health hazard to the residents.

The factor emits smoke day and night and thus pollutes the whole atmosphere. this smoke is very injurious to the health of the residents of this area. Many persons have complained of respiratory and other diseases caused by the smoke pollution.

I, on behalf of the residents of this residential area, request the authorities to pay urgent attention to this problem. It would be better if the factory were shifted from here. Or as an alternative, the factory owners should use smokeless fuel for the factory.

Yours Sincerely,

Kim Yung Lee

Naresh Aggarwal
432 Girgit Street
Lucknow

February 12, ...

The Editor
The Pioneer
Lucknow

Sir

Kindly allow me some space in your esteemed newspaper in order to bring to the notice of the authorities and common people a very urgent social problem afflicting the residents of Girgit Nagar, Lucknow.

Recently, a wine shop has been opened near our locality. The opening of the wine shop in close proximity to this colony is not only strange but against rules also. According to the rules, the opinion of the residents of colony should be obtained before opening a wine shop near that colony. If people object to the opening of such a shop, it will not be opened. But in case of this wine shop, our opinion was not sought. It is believed that the wine shop has been opened by someone who is close to the authorities and so the rules concerning the opening of a wine shops have been ignored.

The opening of the wine shop has proved to be a big nuisance. Day and night, we find a huge rush of drunkards and anti-social elements at the shop. These people uses foul language and pass dirty remarks to the passers by, particularly women. It has become difficult for women to come out of their homes in the evening. The presence of a wine shop has a bad influence on young boys and children also. Very often, there are drunken brawls around the shop.

Therefore, I request the concerned authorities to pay a serious attention to this evil. They should visit to this area and see the things for themselves. I suggest that the wine shop should be shifted to a place away from the residential colony.

Thanking you

Sincerely yours

Naresh Aggarwal

C.G. Verghese
34 Shayam Estate
Bangalore

September 10, ...

The Editor
The Times of India
New Delhi

Sir

Through your newspaper, I wish to draw the attention of the public to the growing interference of politicians in the matters of transfers and appointments of public servants. Nepotism in such matters has become a rule rather than exception. If there is even a single vacancy in a government department, the politicians consider it their birth right to get some of their relatives adjusted there. Cases of corruptions among politicians have also come to light. Many times, they take bribe from the poor unemployed youth with the promise of giving them a job. As a result, the vacancy is not filled on the basis of real merit. Non-deserving persons get the job while the deserving candidates have to run from pillar to post in search of jobs.

Similar is the case with transfer of government employees. The politicians get active when the season of transfers comes. Every politician is interested in getting the man of his choice appointed. They are busy if either punishing the errant employee by getting them transferred to non-profitable areas, or benefitting some faithful person by getting him transferred to a good post. A number of politicians accept bribes also from people to get them transferred to the stations of their choice. The large scale corruption has affected the efficiency of the employees.

It is high time that adequate and timely steps were taken to check the interference of politicians in public appointments and transfers.

Yours sincerely,

C.G. Verghese

Richard Johnson
356 Lawyers Colony
Ankola

April 15, ...

The Editor
The Statesman
Ankola

Sir

I wish to highlight a common malaise through the columns of your newspaper. Strikes and demonstrations have become an order of the day in our country. The workers, the government servants, the traders, the rickshaw pullers — in fact, people in all walks of society — often resort to strikes and demonstrations to highlight their genuine or baseless demands. People often try to solve their minor problems through strikes, demonstrations etc. Slogan shouting and defying the authorities have become very common. People are ready to go on strikes even on the slightest of excuses. Those who resort to these practices do not understand how much inconvenience is caused to the general public.

In a number of cases, the strikers become violent and the police has to use force or tear gas in order to disperse them. After the firing, the enquiry commissions are appointed to look into the causes of violence. Thus, a lot of money is spent which simply goes down the drain.

Ankola is a developing economy. What we need is a joint and concerted effort to make it a buoyont and leading economy. We cannot afford the luxury of strikes and demonstrations. A great number of man-days are lost every year because of these strikes.

I suggest that the government should take a stern view of these strikes and bandhs. There should be a ban on all kinds of strikes and demonstrations. At least the strike in essential services like medical, educations, transport, and banking should be completely banned. The government should appoint high power tribunals to look into the problems and grievances of the common people issue. Anti-social elements should not be allowed to take the law in their own hands.

Yours sincerely

Richard Johnson

V. John
Diamond Enclace
Bombay

March 18, ...

The Editor
The National Herald
New Delhi

Sir

Though the columns of your esteemed newspaper, I wish to highlight a grievance of our village. There is an urgent need of opening a dispensary in village Shamlon Kalan. Ours is a big village with a population of about ten thousand. But there is no dispensary in this village. People have to go to the Bilaspur village dispensary even for the treatment of minor diseases. People face real difficulty when there is an emergency case as the Bilaspur village dispensary is 15 kilometers away. The problem becomes more acute in the rainy season.

As there is no dispensary, the unqualified doctors and quacks have a field day in our village. Only last week a man died in our village as no qualified doctor was available in the village and an unqualified one failed to given him even the proper first aid.

Therefore, on behalf of the people of this village, I request the health authorities to open a dispensary in this village immediately.

Yours sincerely

V. John

P. Vichai
128, Azad Mahad
Bangkok
September 12, ...

The Editor
The Nation
Bangkok

Sir

Kindly allow me to draw, through the columns of your newspaper, the attention of the public towards a great social nuisance. This is the nuisance of begging in the streets and trains.

Begging has been present in our country since ancient times, but now it has assumed the proportion of a big evil. Once a foreigner remarked the symbol of Thailand is an outstretched hand. You can find beggars swarming every public place. Whether you go to the market or the temple, you will find yourselves surrounded by hordes of beggars. You will find them on the railway platforms and in the trains. They even pester you in streets and call at your doorsteps to beg for alms.

Begging is a blot on the name of Thailand. The worst thing is that among the beggars there are many men and women who are quite hale and hearty but they indulge in begging because they are shirkers and do not want to labour. In some cities, the beggars are organised in a kind of Mafia and keep on recruiting new beggars to their ranks. In some cases, these beggars indulge in crime like stealing, shoplifting or even murders. Some beggars kidnap young children, mutilate their limbs and force them to beg.

I, therefore, request the authorities that the menace of begging should be firmly checked. The really disabled and weak persons should be helped by the government so that they do not have to beg.

Yours sincerely

P. Vichai

Mizra Asaf Ali
346, Kotputli Lane
Sholapur (Mah.)

September 10, ...

The Editor
The Times of India
Mumbai

Sir

Kindly let me express my views, through the columns of your esteemed Daily on a matter of profound significance. The modern society is becoming more and more faithless. The religious and moral values which were the mainstay of the Indian society are fast giving place to the materialistic values. This lack of morality, faith and ethics is visible in every field, whether it is business, politics, or society in general. Most of the social ills present today are because of the separation of morality or faith from life.

I am, therefore, of the opinion (and feel that every right thinking Indian will agree with me) that there is an urgent need of introducing moral education in schools. Childhood or boyhood is an impressionable age. This is an age when anything taught to a person is imprinted on his mind almost permanently. The things learned at this stage have a great bearing upon a person's future behaviour. Therefore, a child should be taught the good things of life.

Unfortunately, in the name of secularism, we have done away with moral education in schools and colleges. However, the moral education need not be the education about one religion. A child can be taught good things of life without teaching him any particular religion. The syllabus of moral education may include all the good things of life without necessarily including any particular religion. The child should be taught to give equal respect to all religions; he should be told the importance of faith, honesty, fair dealing, abstinence, etc. Haryana has taken lead in this matter and a separate paper of moral education has been included in the course curriculum upto the senior secondary level. It is time, the whole country followed suit and introduced moral education in the syllabi of different universities.

I proposed that at least one period daily should be devoted to moral education. This will go a long way in tackling the malaise that is afflicting us at the present time.

Yours sincerely

Mizra Asaf Ali

Rajneesh Behl
Dept. of English
Govt. College
Jind (Hry)

November 18, ...

The Editor
The Hindustan Times
New Delhi

Sir

Through the columns of your newspaper, I wish to express my views on the importance of N.C.C. training in schools and colleges. It is a pity that the value of NCC training for students is not being sufficiently recognised by the general public and even by the educational authorities. NCC training for students has acquired supreme importance in the context of the situation prevailing at present in our country.

The defence of the country is of paramount importance. Unfortunately, we not have good relations with Pakistan and China and both these countries have invaded India in the past. Although our armed forces are fully capable of meeting any challenge, yet the NCC trained students can prove very useful as reserved force, as is the case in some countries.

Even if there is no war, NCC training can serve a useful purpose. The NCC training has a great character building effect on youngmen and women. The virtues of discipline, obedience, team work and mutual cooperation are instilled into the NCC cadets. Discipline and a sense of dedication to the nation are the crying needs of our country at present. Realising the importance of the compulsory for students. While one cannot agree to this suggestion, yet the importance of NCC cannot be overlooked. Efforts should be made to attract more and more students to join the NCC. They should be educated about the benefits of NCC training for an individual as well for the nation. The government too should provide adequate facilities for NCC training in schools and colleges of the country.

Yours sincerely
Rajneesh Behl

Rohan Kanitkar
328, Malviya Colony
Yangoon

December 12, ...

The Editor
national Herald
Yangoon

Sir

Kindly allow me to draw the attention of the authorities of the municipality of Yangoon to the deplorable condition of Malviya Colony. there is utter lack of civic amenities in this big colony of Yangoon. The roads of the colony are in a deplorable condition. There are big pot holes on the roads which are health hazards in two ways. In the rainy season, these pot holes are filled with water and become breeding grounds for mosquitoes and flies. Secondly they make driving very difficult and have caused a number of accidents. These roads appear to be roads of the nineteenth century and not the Myanmar which is preparing to go into the twenty first century.

There is absence of street light in the colony. Most of the poles in the colony remain without bulbs and tubes for most part of the year. The dark streets are a great encouragement to the thieves and other anti-social elements.

The streets are of the colony are not properly and frequently cleaned. The sweepers assigned to this colony do not perform their duty well and there seems to be no one to check them. Heaps of rubbish can be seen lying here and there which not only look unseemly, but also spread disease.

I, therefore request the Municipal authorities on behalf of the residents of the colony to take immediate steps for the improvement of the colony.

Yours sincerely

Rohan Kanitkar

S. Murugaswami
54 Kamraj Colony
Penang

May 3, ...

The Editor
The Hindu
Kasturi Building
Penang

Sir

Through the columns of your newspaper, I wish to draw the attention of the Municipality Corporation of Penang to the scarcity of drinking water in our colony. The problem becomes severe in the summer season. But this summer, it has become very acute. A lot of water is needed in every household in such season. But for the last two months the residents of our colony have been facing great scarcity. We get water supply only for one hour in the morning and one in the evening. This is not sufficient to meet the needs of even a moderate sized family. During these two hours of water supply also, the pressure of water is so low that it does not reach even the first floor of a house.

Thus, people are having a tough time during this summer. Sometimes people have to go without bath for two or three days in a stretch. The Municipal Corporation is requested to pay urgent attention to the inconvenience of the general public and ensure better and regular water supply.

Yours sincerely

S. Murugaswami

XIII. BANKING CORRESPONDENCE

135. Request for an overdraft or loan

Dr. Graham Greene
238 Riverside
London

June 23, ...

The Manager
Morgan Stanley Bank
Queens Building
Cathays Park
London

Dear Sir

I am a doctor by profession and I have my clinic at 238, Riverside.
I have a good practice and my monthly income is more than 10,000
pounds. Now I want to expand my clinic and provide more facilities
to the patients. I wish to purchase an X-Ray plant and an ultra-sound
scan instrument for my clinic. The total expenses involved is this
purchase are about one hundred thousand pounds.

I request you to grant me a loan of eighty thousand pounds for this
purpose. I am prepared to mortgage my clinic for securing this loan.
The present value of my clinic is about two hundred thousands pounds.
Apart from mortgaging the clinic, I am prepared to provide two
guarantors which would testify as to my character and paying capacity.

I hope you would accede to my request for granting me the loan.

Yours faithfully,

Graham Greene

MORGAN STANLEY BANK

Queens Building
Cathays Park
London

June 27, ...

Dr. Graham Greene
238 Riverside
London

Dear Dr. Greene

With reference to your letter of 23rd June, I am pleased to inform you that a loan of 80 thousand pounds as requested by you has been approved by our main office.

This loan has been approved subject to the condition that you will mortgage your Clinic with all its equipment to the bank. The loan carries the interest at the prevailing rate of 11 per cent which will be calculated on half yearly basis.

Kindly visit the bank on 30th June to complete the formalities of granting the loan to you.

Thanking you

Yours sincerely

Richard White
Manager

MORGAN STANLEY BANK

Queens Building
Cathays Park
London

June 27, ...

Dr. Graham Greene
238 Riverside
London

Dear Dr. Greene

Kindly refer to your letter of 23rd June. I am sorry to inform you that we will not be able to give you the loan of eighty thousand pounds as requested by you. There are two reasons behind our not accepting to your request.

The security offered by you for this loan is not sufficient. Secondly, there is a credit squeeze at present which has particularly affected loans. I sympathise with you because you need this loan for upgrading the facilities at your clinic which will be beneficial for the general public. But our bank's policies at present do not allow us to grant you this loan.

I am sorry that we have to disappoint you in this matter and hope that we may be of more help in the future. I hope you will be able to arrange loan from some other source.

Yours sincerely

Richard White
Manager

PUNJAB NATIONAL BANK

Sector 17
Chandigarh

August 17, ...

Mr. D.K. Singh
Director
Dara Studio
Chandigarh

Dear Mr. Singh

You will be glad to know that a new branch of our bank, The Punjab National Bank has been opened just opposite your film Studio. The bank will be open on all days from 10 a.m. to 2 p.m. for public transactions. The bank will be open on Sundays but will remain closed on every Tuesday.

Courtesy and efficiency are the hall marks of our bank. Customer satisfaction is our motto. We have a number of attractive deposit schemes for public. We request you to open your current and saving accounts at our bank and also bring us deposits in the form of fixed deposits. You are requested to meet me any time during working ours so that I can explain the bank's attractive schemes to you in detail.

Thanking you,

Yours sincerely

K.L. Miglani
Senior Manager

Jameela
458, Jalan Bejing
Kaula Lumper

July 13, ...

The Manager
Chartered Bank
Jalan Masjid
Kuala Lumpur

Sir

I have joined the head office. I am joining my new office after about one week. I therefore, request you to kindly transfer my account No. 3474 to Standard Bank, Jalan Masjid, India, Kuala Lumper.

Thank you,

Yours sincerely

Jameela

Zubair Mohammed
23 Jhanj Gate
Singapore

September 18, ...

The Manager
Bank of Tokyo
Orchard Road
Singapore

Subject : Request for a locker facility

Sir

I want to keep some bonds, ornaments and valuable papers in safe custody. For this I need a locker in your bank. You are requested kindly to inform me whether lockers are available at your bank.

Kindly also let me know what formalities I would be required to undergo for availing myself of this facility.

Thanking you

Yours sincerely

Zubair Mohammed

KETSONS BOOK SHOP

G-10 South Extension
Hong Kong

April 12, ...

The Manager
City Bank
Main Road
Hong Kong

Dear Sir

I have just been informed by M/s Paper Mills, Hong Kong that my cheque No. 8764 for $5,600/- issued to them on 5th April has been refused payment by you. Your bank has given the reason, 'not enough balance' for refusing payment.

This reason is quite absurd. When my previous cheque, that is, cheque no. 8763 was cleared for payment about a month back, the balance in my account was 45,000/-. Thereafter I deposited $13,000 in cash and also deposited a cheque for $4,450 (No. 2365 dated 10th March, drawn at State Bank) which should have been cleared by now.

So, it is not clear why my cheque has been dishonoured. You are requested kindly to look into the matter. In the mean time, I am sending the cheque back to the concerned firm for deposit in your bank once again.

Kindly keep me abreast of the decision taken by you in this regard.

Yours faithfully

Iqbal Masud
(Managing Director)

XIV. CIRCULARS, APPLICATIONS, FOR LOANS, LEAVES AND REQUESTS

142. Circular for Independence Day celebrations

CENTRAL BOARD OF SCHOOL EDUCATION

16 Chitragupta Road
New Delhi

January 16, ...

To

The Principles of
All Senior Secondary Schools
New Delhi

Sir/Madam

This is to bring to your kind notice that the Central Board of School Education has decided that Independence Day will be celebrated in every school in Delhi which comes under the CBSE.

As it is a national holiday, there will be no teaching work in the schools. But the staff members and the students will be asked to come on 15th August and take part in the Independence Day celebrations. The Principal of each school will make arrangements for unfurling the national flag in the school. Thereafter, the school shall hold a celebration which will include songs, drama, etc. Each Principal will chalk out the programme for celebration in the way he/she likes best.

After the celebration, each principal shall forward a report to the undersigned regarding the function.

R. K. Desai

Director

OFFICE OF THE VICE-CHANCELLOR
CHULANGKORN UNIVERSITY, BANGKOK

September 10, ...

To

      The Heads of all Teaching
      departments & Superintendents
      of All Administrative offices
      Chulangkorn University
      Bangkok

It has come to my notice that several members of the teaching staff of this university as well the members of the administrative staff are not punctual in their duties. They are consistently late on one pretext or the other. I have observed a number of teachers of the university and found most of them coming late to meet their classes in the first period. Sometimes, they miss their first period altogether. This is a serious matter as the students suffer for no fault of theirs.

In the same way I found the members of the clerical or administrative staff late in reporting to their work in the morning. I am taking a serious view of this matter and feel that this practice should be curbed at once. The Heads of departments and the superintendents/Incharges of administrative offices of the university must ensure that the teachers/employees working under them are do not report late to their work. In future, all such cases of negligence will be dealt with severely.

Each member of the teaching/administrative staff must mark the time of his arrival and departure in the registers maintained for this purpose.

Vice-Chancellor

October 18, ...

To

      The Under Secretary
      Ministry of Agriculture
      Govt. of Malaysia
      Kuala Lumpur

Sir

I have been working as a Stenographer in the Ministry of Agriculture for the last fifteen years. I am a dedicated worker and my officers have spoken highly of my efficiency and devotion to work. I have still fifteen years of service left.

The marriage of my daughter has been fixed for 15th December, that is, about two months from now. I do not have much of bank balance and am facing difficulty in making arrangements for the marriage. You are requested kindly to sanction a loan of Ringet 50,000 out of my Provident Fund. This will greatly help me in meeting the marriage expenses.

The loan may please be deducted from my salary in equal installments till my time of retirement.

Thanking you in anticipation,

Yours faithfully

Ishaq Mohammad
Stenographer

Secretary
Salem Steel Corporation
Employees' Union

May 18, ...

The Managing Director
Salem Steel Corporation
Salem

Subject : Notice for strike

Sir

The workers of the Salem Steel Corporation have been trying to get their legitimate demands met for the last one year. They have made a number of representations to the management during this period. But the management has either ignored these demands or has given some half-hearted promises. But the demands have remained unmet.

Therefore, I, on behalf of the Union, hereby give you this notice that if our demands are not met by 20th May, we will be compelled to go on indefinite strike from 21st May. I give below the list of demands once again :

1. Payment of bonus for the previous year which has not been paid to them.

2. Revision of pay scales by at least 40 percent as the prices have increased manifold during the last few years.

3. Better service and living conditions such as better insurance cover for deaths and injuries during the last few years.

4. Living quarters for all the employees.

5. Facility of leave travel concession.

6. Full reimbursement of medical expenses.

Mustaq Ahamed

Secretary
SSC Employees Union

SALEM STEEL CORPORATION

217 Steel Nagar
Salem

May 19, ...

Mr. Mushtaq Ahmed
Secretary
SS Employees' Union
Salem

Dear Mr. Mushtaq Ahmed,

This has a reference to your notice conveying the decision of the SS Employees Union to go on indefinite strike on the matter of your demands. Let me point out that your decision to go on strike is contrary to labour laws because the wage structure was revised two years ago and the general rule stipulates that a status quo in wage structure can be maintained for three years.

You must be aware that the rule "no work no pay" apply to those workers who abstain from work. The workers will not be paid any salary for the day(s) they remain on strike. Your decision will hit hard the poorer sections of the workers. I know that a majority of workers are not in favour of going on strike and therefore, we have informed the police to deal firmly with those who prevent the faithful workers from entering the premises or from doing their duties. The police has been asked to use force if the situation becomes worse. Hence, any injury to your colleagues owing their misbehaviour will be your responsibility.

Yours sincerely,

Harold Jackson
Managing Director

November 18, ...

To

    The General Manager
    Diana Heavy Electricals
    Glasgow

        Subject : Leave for my sister's marriage

Sir

The marriage of my sister has been fixed for the 29th of this month. As my father is not alive and I am the eldest member of my family, the whole responsibility of her marriage is on my shoulders. I have to make all the arrangements for the marriage.

You are, therefore, requested kindly to grant me leave for ten days from 21st 30th November. As I have already exhausted by casual leave, I may be given earned leave for this period.

Thanking you

Yours faithfully

Steve Jack
Senior Accountant

August 18, ...

To

The General Manager
Panton Potteries Ltd.
Glasgow (UK)

Sir,

Subject : Compensation Increase Request

I have been thinking for some time to request you to raise my salary. First I wish to reaffirm my value to the Hitkari Potteries. I want to draw attention to my accomplishments and my contribution to the development of this company.

I joined this firm ten years ago and during this period, all my colleagues and seniors have found me hard working and sincere. I have always considered this company as a family and the employees as its members with each employee working towards its betterment. It was because of my untiring efforts and resourcefulness that I got a number of orders for the company. I hope, you will not undermine my services in the commissioning of the new pottery plant at Bahadurgarh.

Next, I wish to remind you gently that my salary has not been increased for three years. Inflaction continues to increase, and money does not go as far as it once did. Therefore, I request you for a revaluation of my total wage package, trusting that my value as an employee and team member would be reflected in a well-deserved increase. I know that it is unnecessary for me to dwell much on my services. As a good administrator you keep a watch over the work of each one of us and are very familiar with my work habits and my dedication to the company.

I hope my request for an increase in the salary would be favourably considered.

Thanking you

Yours faithfully

John Lyndon
Asstt. Manager

XV. SCHOOL, COLLEGE AND UNIVERSITY CORRESPONDENCE

---

149. Application for Child's admission

Nitish Bhardwaj
295/5 Housing Board Colony
Hyderabad.

June 15, ...

To

The Principal
Happly Dales Public School
Civil Lines
Seccunderabad

Sir

I wish to admit my son Shubham, who is four years old, to your renowned public school.

My son has a more than average IQ for a child of four years and I am sure, he will bring laurels to your school. I am employed as Lecturer in English at Arts College, Osmania University, Hyderabad and my wife is a senior teacher at a government school. Thus there is an educational environment conducive to the study of my son. We both being in teaching profession, have ample time at our disposal to devote to his homework and other educational needs.

Kindly give my son a chance to sit for the interview and entrance test.

Thanking you,

Yours sincerely

(Nitish Bhardwaj)

July 19, ...

To

The Principal
Harrow Public School
Bangkok

Subject : Request for Stipend

Sir

I am a student of class XI of your school. I have been in this school for the last three years. As you can find from the school records, I have been one of the outstanding students of the school. I have consistently been among the best three students of the class since I joined this school. Apart from this, I take a keen interest in extra-curricular activities like sports, declamation, singing etc. Last year I was awarded the All Rounder's Shield. I am captain of the hockey team of my House.

My father is employed as a Clerk in a government department. We are a family of five members and it is difficult for him to meet my study expenses. I am enclosing with this application, the salary certificate of my father. It is particularly difficult for me to pay the hiked science laboratory fees.

Therefore, I request you to kindly sanction a suitable stipend for me to permit to continue my studies.

I shall remain obliged to you for this act of kindness.

Thanking you in anticipation,

Yours obediently

John Russel
(Roll No. 327 Class XI)

OFFICE OF THE PRINCIPAL
SHIVALIK PUBLIC SCHOOL
(Kuala Lumpur)

March 12, ...

To
Arun Bhagat
Class VIII

You have not improved despite numerous warnings given to you by me and your class teachers. Your misconduct in the school still continues. Many teachers have complained about your aggressive behaviour with the class mates. At a number of times you have shown disrespect to your teachers also. You were let off in the past with light punishments because you had promised to reform yourself. But I find that your promise was not at all genuine. Yesterday, you struck Manoj of class VII with your cricket bat and injured him seriously. Such a behaviour cannot be tolerated.

I am, therefore, compelled to rusticate you from the school with immediate effect. Your parents have also been informed.

Principal

Shivalik Public School

LITTLE ANGELS PUBLIC SCHOOL
(Colombo)

July 27, ...

To

      All the parents/guardians
      of the students of class VII

Dear parent/guardian

It is to inform you that the Parent-Teacher Meet for Class VII in which your ward studies has been fixed for 1st August, ... This is an important meeting in which the class teachers will discuss with you, your ward's merits and shortcomings. At the same time, you may also air your views/grievances/suggestions at the meeting.

You are requested to make it convenient to attend this meeting. Your cooperation will greatly help us in our task of providing high class education to your child.

With best regards,

Sincerely yours

Col. Sudhu Ranaratne (Retd.)
Principal

LUDLOW PUBLIC SCHOOL
(Singapore)

November 10, ...

To

The parents/guardians of
the students of this school

Dear Parents

You will be glad to know that the Annual Day Function of the Ludlow Public School, Singapore will be held on the 20th of this month. This year's Annual Day Function has a special significance as on this day we are celebrating the golden jubilee of the school. A big cultural show will be organised on this day to mark this occasion.

I, on behalf of the management, staff and students of this school, invite you to attend this function at the School auditorium. Your presence will encourage us in our endeavours to provide quality education to your wards.

Thanking you

Yours sincerely

M. Moris
Principal

February 12, ...

To

The Librarian
Jesus and Mary Postgraduate College
Amsterdam

Sir,

I am a student of B.A. Hons (English) of this college. I borrowed two books from the college two months ago. Then there were three holidays in the college. I went to London to visit my uncle and took the books with me. By mistake I forgot the books there. I came to know of this mistake when I came back to Amsterdam. But by that time my uncle had left for America and returned only last week. Then he sent the books to me by post.

Today, when I came to library to return the books, I found that a late return fine of Gilder 100/- on the books is due from me.

Sir, my father is a man of limited means. This fine will be a strain on his resources. So, you are requested kindly to remit this fine.

Thanking you in anticipation,

Yours obediently

Dorothy D'Souza
B.A. Hons (English)

September 19, ...

To

The Principal
Jamsher College
Kuala Lumpur

Sir

I am a student of Manik College, Sabah in B.Sc. (IInd year). My father, who is in the Irrigation department has been transferred to Kuala Lumpur. It is difficult for me continue my studies at Sabah. So I wish to migrate to your college. According to the university rules, the consent of the principal of the college where a student wishes to migrate is required first.

So, you are requested kindly to allow me to migrate to your college in B.Sc (II year). I have been one of the outstanding students of Manik College, Sabah. I have scored one of the top three positions for the last three years. I hope, you will allow me to join your prestigious college.

Thanking you

Yours obediently

A. Minna
B.Sc. (II year)

OFFICE OF THE PRINCIPAL
NARSEE MONJEE COLLEGE OF COMMERCE
(Berlin)

October 15, ...

NOTICE

The students and the staff of the Narsee Monjee College of Commerce are hereby informed that the elections to the Students Council of the College will be held on 28th of this month. The elections will be for the following offices of the Students Council :

(a)	President	One
(b)	Vice-President	One
(c)	Secretary	One
(d)	Joint Secretary	One
(e)	Treasurer	One
(f)	Class representatives	One from each class

The elections will be held as per the following schedule :

1.	The last date for filing the nomination for various offices.	17th November
2.	The last date for withdrawing the candidate	20th November
3.	The date of scrunity of forms	21st November
4.	Announcement of the candidates elegible for contesting	22nd November
5.	Date of Election	28th November

Prof. G.S. Mahanobolis, Head, Department of Political Science will act as In-charge for these elections. All the queries regarding the elections should also be addressed to him.

V.K. Hopes

Principal

October 08, ...

To

   The Principal
   St. Mary College
   New York

Madam,

I, on behalf of the students of this college, bring to your kind notice the far from satisfactory condition of the college library. A library is the heart of a college. If this is not functioning properly, the college can be said to be functioning in a lop-sided manner. Unfortunately, the library of this college leaves much to be desired.

The college library is ill-stocked. The Reference section is particularly famished and the most common reference books in many subjects are not available in the college library. The students have often to depend on other libraries for their needs. And for this purpose they spend a lot of time and money also.

Apart from the books, there are other ills plaguing the library. There are not enough number of tables in the reading room where students can read newspapers and periodicals. Also, there should be more tables in the stack hall where students can study books and make notes from them. The library does not follow the open-shelf system and the students have to approach the librarian even if he has only to browse through a book.

The students hope that you will kindly look into the matter and solve our problems.

Thanking you,

Yours obediently

Philomena Rose
President, Students Union

OFFICE OF THE PRINCIPAL
ST. STEPHEN'S COLLEGE
(Chicago)

February 15, ...

NOTICE

It is for the information of the staff members and students of the St. Stephen's College that the 26th Annual Athletic Meet of the College will be held in the College Stadium on 27 and 28th February. Those students who wish to take part in various athletic events, may give their names to Mr. J.R. Vaidya the Director of Physical Education of this college by the 20th of this month.

Apart from the athletic events for the students, there will be a musical chair race item for the staff and guests on the final day of the meet. There will be a three-legged race for the teaching and administerial staff. A pitcher race will be organised for the wives of the teaching staff. In this race, the participants will run with earthen pitchers on their heads. Whosoever reaches the finishing line first and with the pitcher (not to be supported by hands) intact, will be the winner.

The students are requested to participate in the athletic meet with enthusiasm.

B. George
Principal

XVI. CORRESPONDENCE REGARDING INSURANCE

159. *Request for Accidental Insurance*

SHERLOCK HOLMES RACING CLUB

Queens Hill
29 Haltwhistle
Northumber land

May 12, ...

The General Manager
Callagham Insurance Co.
Society House
Manchester

Dear Sir

This racing club which was established four months ago is planning to take part in the cross-country motor racing competition which is held every year and which covers a distance of 1000 kms. across some of the roughest terrains. As many as 10 of our members will be taking part in the motor race.

Kindly let us know if you have any accident insurance policy which can insure these ten of our members against any injury during the race. If there is a policy which meets our needs, would you kindly send your representative to complete the formalities of insurance ?

Thank you,

Yours sincerely

Chinston Wurchill
President

TULLIVER AND WAKEM INSURANCE CO. LTD.

23 Maggie Street
St. Ogg-upon-Floss (UK)

January 05, ...

Mrs. Targaret Matcher
18, Brockleway Road
Leeds (UK)

Dear Mrs. Matcher

Re : Your Policy No. 668-K004

We have received your claim form no. 4591 in which you have claimed 1680 pounds for damage caused to your house when the roof of one of the rooms caved in.

While I sympathise with you for your loss, I regret to say that the loss suffered by you lies beyond the terms of the policy. Hence, we cannot compensate you for your loss. Clause no. 18-a clearly states that the loss to the structure of the house can be compensated if it is due to natural causes. In your case, the roof of the room caved while you were demolishing the adjoining room. The loss is clearly due to the negligence of your engineer.

If you wish, we can send an agent who will explain the policy to you carefully, and if you wish, offer you a new and comprehensive house protection policy.

Yours sincerely

Bony Tlair
Claims Manager

Vinod Rathor
209, Vasant Vihar
New Delhi

February 14, ...

To

The General Manager
The Life Insurance Corporations of India
New Delhi

Subject : General information about insurance policies

Sir,

I and some friends of mine wish to take life insurance policies. So, I would like to have general information about all the different schemes offered by the LIC. This may include schemes for life insurance with general risk cover for all kinds of deaths, e.g. natural, accidental or due to violence.

Kindly send details about insurance policies having provisions for the education and marriage of children and also for house loans.

Thanking you

Yours sincerely

Vinod Rathor

Hrishikesh Mukerjee
128 Shakespeare Sarani
Calcutta

May 16, ...

To

The Manager
LIC of India
Calcutta,

Subject : Renewal of Policy No. 170016089

Sir

I took the above mentioned life insurance policy about three years ago. But owing to some domestic problems I have not been able to pay the regular premiums for the last eighteen months as a result of which the policy has been discontinued.

Now, as my circumstances have eased, I am in a position to pay the premiums on the policy. I, therefore, request you to kindly renew my policy.

Kindly let me know what is the procedure for getting this done and what fine I would have to pay in addition to the previus premiums.

Thanking you

Yours sincerely

Hrishikesh Mukherjee

Haseena Begum
45 Tripolia Road
Jurasalam

March 18, ...

To

The Branch Manager
LIC of Israel
Jursalam

Subject : Claim on premature death

Sir

My husband Mr. Mohammed Kasim Assistant Manager, Chambal Fertilizers, Jurasalam, has an LIC policy (No. 5987721, sum assured : 2,00,000) in his name. He had an massive heart attack while coming from London to Jurasalam on the 8th of this month and died at once on landing.

I am sending herewith the requisite maturity claim form. A death certificate from the Senior Medial Officer of the Civil Hospital is attached herewith.

I am a nominee for the above said policy of my husband. Secondly, I am the legal heir of all his property, according to his will, a copy of which is attached herewith. You are requested to expedite the final claim settlement of this policy. An early claim settlement will be highly appreciated.

Thanking you,

Yours sincerely

Haseena Begum

H.G. Kulkarni
21 Bhagyanagar
Nadiad (Mah.)

June 20, ...

The Branch Manager
LIC of India
Nadiad (Mah.)

Subject : Claim for matured Policy No. 7698431

Sir

My LIC Policy No. 7698431 (policy named Jeevan Suraksha, for insured amount 1,50,000) has matured on the 18th of this month. The maturity amount of Rs. 1,50,00 and the bonus accrued thereon may kindly be disbursed to me at an early date.

Kindly make the payment by cheque or draft. The cheque/draft should be crossed 'payee's account' and should be sent to me by registered post in order to avoid the possibility of its being lost in the transit.

An early action in the matter will be highly appreciated.

Thanking you,

Yours Sincerely

H.G. Kulkarni

Personal
Letters

XVII. LETTERS OF LOVE, COURTSHIP AND MARRIAGE

---

165. Letter of courtship (letter expressing love)

Romeo Bhardwaj
275/5 Lover Locality
Paris
Tel : 65432

March 2, ...

Dearest Madona,

I thank God that he sent you in this world. Otherwise, I would have thought that the whole world was devoid of beauty. My love for you has come as a complete surprise. Browning says, "God creates the love to fulfil the love." After meeting you I have started believing that you were sent in this world to fulfil the love in my heart. I wish I could show you just one portion or one tenth of my heart, to explain the glorious passion I have for you.

Your eyes are so deep and beautiful that when you look into my eyes, I am lost in their depth. For you and our love I try to be my very best, respecting the delicacy of life's treasure, that is our love. Thanking my God for our love, I shed tears and pray that love works in the most supreme of ways. I will never forget our meeting of yesterday when flowing down the stream of passion, you too murmured sweet notings which undoubtedly meant that you too loved me.

I look forward to more frequent meetings so that I am not very far away you, the jewel of my heart, the peace of my mind and the vision of my eyes.

I love you,

Yours and only yours

Stave Maclean

Madona
Queens Park,
Paris

March 6, ...

My dearest Maclean

It was a pleasant surprise when I received your letter. Believe me when your letters reached me I was thinking about you only. Your letter was a fulfilment of heart's deepest desire, that is, to have a positive response to my longing for you.

In the past few days we have come closer. How quickly has our love progressed ! I remember our first meeting in the library when I could not locate a book and you offered to find it out for me. Then our accidental collision and your unwittingly giving me a memory. With the grace of God we had another chance of meeting only two days later and your eyes had told me of your feelings for me. And then a week later came our next meeting when we were along in the lift and your inarticulate and spontaneous expression of love was followed by your tight embrace. For a moment I stiffened but then as I felt the joy of heaven, I too embraced you.

I agree with you that our meetings should be more frequent. I am really waiting for you with a throbbing heart.

Yours for ever

Madona

Madona
123 Querrs Park
March 6, ...

Mr. Steve Maclean

Your love letter came as a great surprise to me. At the same time it filled me with anger at your stupidity in thinking that I was in love with you. Because of the nature of our jobs we have to work in the same office and for the last one week after the change in the office set up, my desk too has come near yours. But this does not mean that my heart too has come closer to yours. In fact, I have some aversion for you and have taken a strong exception to your writing me a love letter. I hope you will not repeat this folly in future.

Let me once again remind that I have no place for you in my heart. I, therefore, request you not to harbour any misunderstanding in your mind about me.

Madona

Alka Deshpandey
39 Brahma Nagar
Kanpur

July 10, ...

Baldev,

I regret to inform you that I have to take the unpleasant decision to break off our relations. I know that I encouraged you by positively responding to your love. But now I feel that my infatuation for you was the impulse of a moment. It was because of the natural instinct of human beings who seek fulfilment in the opposite sex. I was fascinated by your dashing personality and your achievements in the sports.

However, as I got to know you better, many unpleasant facts have come before me. I have come to know that you have ditched two girls after promising to marry them. A reliable person told me that you have been indicted in a case of drug taking and molestation. You promised to make me your life-partner but hid these facts from me. I feel that a momentary suffering is better than the suffering of life time. That is why, I have decided to have nothing to do with you from now onwards.

I wish that you would not write me any letters or try to meet me in future.

Alka Deshpandey

Wanted a match for a beautiful Punjabi girl. Very fair, slim, pretty and attractive, height 5'7". Working as a fashion designer in reputed firm, drawing five figure salary. Well versed in homely affairs. Belongs to a decent family; father a retired officer, two brothers doctors. Caste no bar, preference for match in good service—doctor, engineer or civil servant; or a high class businessman. Apply in detail with photographs to post box no. 10265-CA, C/O Hindustan Times, New Delhi.

B.K. Batra
321, Sector 23-C
Chandigarh

March 8, ...

The Advertiser
Post Box No. 10265-CA
Hindustan Times
New Delhi.

Sir

I came across your matrimonial ad in the Hindustan Times of yesterday. Your advertisement attracted me as I have a son of marriageable age and I think he has all the requirements you are looking for in your prospective son-in-law. I give below the details about my son :

My son, Ritesh Kumar is a young and fine man of 27 years. He is quite tall, that is, 5 feet and 10 inches. He has a healthy body and his weight is ideal according to his height. His complexion is wheatish and his features are sharp.

My son is a B.A. from the Punjab University and an MBA from Ahmedabad. At present he is working as Manager (personnel) with Vimal Textile Mills Ltd. and is posted at Mumbai. He is drawing a salary of Rs. 25,000 per month. Apart from salary, he enjoys attractive perks. My son has good habits and attractive manners.

Ours in a good family. I have retired as a medical officer at the Medical College, Chandigarh. I have three sons and the two beside this one, are in the college. I have one daughter and she is married to an engineer.

I am sending two photographs of my son. If you feel interested in the proposal, kindly let us know and we can discuss the matter still further.

Yours sincerely

B.K. Batra

Shameer Razdaan
48, New Hostel
University of Malaya
Kuala Lumpur

July 20, ...

My Dear Father,

I received your letter today and it brought both the good and bad tidings for me. While I was very happy to learn that Jameela has passed her matriculation examination in Ist division, I had a sense of consternation to learn that you have decided to get me married. You have written that you have a match in mind.

Dear father, I cannot understand the reasons which have prompted you to take such a decision. Moreover, I should have been consulted regarding the time of my marriage. Please do not take this as a disobedience, but I am determined not to marry unless I am able to stand on my own feet. I have a fixed aim before me. I wish to be a university or college lecturer. So, after completing my M.A., I intend to go in for Ph.D in English literature. It is only after getting the job of my liking that I will think of marriage.

In your letter you have desired me to join the family business after completing the M.A. as elder brother Rakesh has done. I know that ours is a flourishing business and my teaching job cannot bring me as much financial benefit as our business can. Yet, I feel that money is not everything in life. A person gets real joy and satisfaction in life only when he was adopted the career of his heart's liking. You have written that you are not able to devote much time to business and want me to join elder brother in running the business. However, you know that brother has proved himself an astute business man. I am confident that under your guidance, he will take our business to new heights. As far as I am concerned, I wish to devote my life to the study of English literature.

So, dear father, I once again request you not to press me for getting married at this stage. I hope, mother also supports me on this point.

With regards to mother,

Yours affectionately
Shameer Razdaan

XVIII. INVITATIONS, THEIR ACCEPTANCE/ NON ACCEPTANCE, ETC.

Mrs. and Mr. Avinash Kumar Khanna

request the pleasure of the company of

Mrs. and Mr. Manonar Varma

on the auspicious occasion of

the marriage of their daughter

Shalini

with

Rakesh

(son of Mrs. and Mr. Raj Kumar Sindwani of Shimla)

at Banquet Hall, Aroma Hotel,

Sector 23, Chandigarh

on 10th November, ... at 7.30 pm.

R.S.V.P.

Avinash Khanna
129 Sector 18-B
Chandigarh

Mrs. and Mr. Manonar Varma

heartily thank

Mrs. and Mr. Avinash Kumar Khanna

for their invitation to the

marriage of their daughter

Shalini

with

Rakesh

but express their inability to attend it

owing to certain other preoccupations.

Please accept our hearty wishes for the newly-wed couple.

Kamla and Monohar Varma
34, Greenpark, New Delhi

N. D'Costa
129 Sector 18-B
Civil Lines,
Manila

November 01, ...

Mr. S. D'Souza
34, Greenpark
Manila

My Dear D'Souza,

This gives me great pleasure to inform you that with the grace of God, the marriage of my daughter Falcy D'Costa has been fixed for the 10th of this month with Mr. George, son of Mrs. and Mr. John of Zurich. My wife and I request the pleasure of your company at this auspicious occasion.

The marriage will be solemnised at Banquet Hall, Aroma Hotel, Sector 23, Manila at 8.30 pm.

Please do attend the marriage along with your family and bless the newly wed couple.

With kind regards,

Sincerely yours
N. D'Costa

S. D'Souza
34, Greenpark, Manila
November 04, ...

Mr. N D'Costa
129 Sector 18-B
Manila

My dear Mr. D'Costa,

It was a pleasant surprise to receive your invitation to the wedding of your daughter Falcy D'Costa. How swiftly the time passes! It appears only a matter of yesterday when dear Falcy (whom we called Rosy) used to speak in a lisping voice and insisted on sitting in my lap. Because of some pressing engagements of life, I have not seen her for a long time. And now it has given great pleasure to find that she has grown up to be of marriageable age and her marriage has been fixed for the 10th of this month.

Dear D'Costa, it goes without saying that I, along with my wife and children, will attend this marriage and bless our dear Rosy. Rather I am eagerly looking forward to attending the wedding ceremony.

Thank you once again and with kind regards,

Sincerely yours

D'Souza

Col. Raj Pal Katyal
569 M.I. Road
Jammu

October 10, ...

Col. D.S. Chaudhary
98/12 Defence Colony
Jammu

My Dear Col. Chaudhary

I am hosting a small cocktail cum dinner party to welcome some foreign guests who are coming to my residence on their visit to India. I have invited some ex-colleagues also and they have conveyed their consent to attend the dinner. I do not disclose their names at yet as it would be a pleasant surprise to you to meet them at my residence after so many years of retirement from active service.

If you are there at the party, we'll together sip our favourite gin and revive the memories of the days gone by. Trust me when I say that your company will enhance the charm of the party manifold.

So, I invite you cordially to grace the dinner party with your charming and vivacious presence.

With kind regards,

Sincerely yours

Col. Raj Pal Katyal

PAWAN KUMAR BANSAL

Senior Correspondent, Indian Express

Cordially invites you to attend the function

to release his latest book

THE PRESS IN INDIA, THREATS AND CHALLENGES

Published by

Goodwill Books (India)

to be released by

Eminent journalist and writer

SH. KULDIP NAYYAR

on

February 18, ... at 6.30 p.m.

at Gandhi Peace Foundation, Near ITO, New Delhi.

Mr. Prabhash Joshi, Editor, Janstatta

will be the Chief Guest

and

Eminent writer and columnist

Khushwant Singh

will be the Chief Speaker

R.S.V.P.

Pawan Kumar Bansal
Indian Express
Bahadurshah Zafar Marg
New Delhi

John Braganza
243, Dalton Avenue
Mauritius

July 18, ...

Mr. Ashok Khemka
65, Model Town
Patna

My Dear Ashok

I hope you have fully recovered from your recent weakness. Last week I received your elder brother's letter which told me that you are in a somewhat depressed mood after your illness. Such moods of depression sometimes visit a man without any reason. But a man of courage like you does not yield to such moods and comes out of them soon.

It is said that change of weather and atmosphere is the best antidote for a depressed mood. Nothing lifts our spirits and cheers them in a better way than a visit to the refreshing climate of hills in summer. Your summer vacations are beginning next month. I invite you to visit Mauritius along with me. Mauritius is called the Heaven on Earth. There is no doubt that this place has breathtaking scenes and invigorating atmosphere.

Please make up your mind to visit this coming beautiful place and let me know when you are reaching Mauritius.

I am looking forward for having a wonderful time in your company.

Yours truly

John Braganza

XIX. LETTERS OF CONGRATULATIONS AND GREETINGS

179. To a friend on success in examination

A. Sethi
275/5 Gandhi Nagar
Jind 126102 (Hry)

March 08, ...

Mr. V.R. Jain
871 Nicholson Road
Ambala (Hry)

Dear Vijay Rishi

Imagine my joy when I read the result of the I.A.S. in the Hindustan Times and found that you had obtained the 2nd rank. Please accept my hear-felt congratulations on your grand success.

This success of yours is well-deserved. I remember the time and energy that you put into your efforts to succeed in this examination. While your other friends whiled away their time in gossip or were sound asleep at night, you were pouring over the bulky books. I remember the golden line which you often quote : "Success in every field is ninety nine per cent perspiration and one per cent inspiration. Your success in your efforts has amply proved the truth of this statement.

When are you coming to Jind ? I have planned a big function to celebrate your success to which all our old friends will be invited.

Congratulations once again,

Yours truly

A. Sethi

Mithilesh Kumar
89 Dharampura
Aligarh

October 10, ...

Mr. Pramesh Gandhi
741 Sherjang Extension
Meerut

Dear Pramesh

My heartiest congratulations on your breaking your vow of celibacy and marrying a pretty girl of your locality. I'm sorry I could not attend your marriage due to my father's illness. However, our friend Dharam Shende who attended you marriage wrote to me about the marriage function.

Dharam happens to know the girl you have married and has written to me about her good qualities and sweet personality. He has also written that you are planning to visit Gangtok to celebrate your honey moon. I wish you a jolly time there and also wish you a long and happy conjugal bliss.

When you return from the honeymoon, do pay us a visit along with your sweet better half. Convey my congratulations and good wishes to her also.

With best regards,

Yours truly

Mithilesh Kumar

Barkat Ali
347 Hazrat Ganj
Lahore

March 12, ...

Mr. Saifuddin Ahmad
129 Raisina Hill
Lahore

Dear Saifuddin

My dearest congratulations at your recovery from a serious disease. According to psychologists and medical men, the effect of medicines is considerably lessened if the patient loses courage in the face of a serious disease and starts thinking that he will not recover. On the other hand, if a patient's will power is strong and he can face disease with courage, the efficacy of medicines is increased manifold and the chances of the patient's recovery are enhanced.

Needless to say that it was your own fortitude and belief in Allah that taught you to face the serious disease bravely. I once again congratulate you.

As you are convalescing from the disease, you must take nutritious food and observe strict care in the matter of food and daily routine. You must consult the doctor daily till you have fully recovered.

Please pay my regards to your parents.

With best regards,

Yours truly

Barkat Ali

P.K. Sethi
237 Begum Bazar
Agra

April 23, ...

Sh. Navjot Sidhu
34 B. Roy Road
Mathura

Dear Navjot

Heartiest congratulations on winning the Rockefeller Foundation scholarship for further studies in the field on Cytology in the USA. This scholarship will fulfil your long standing ambition of undergoing advanced studies in the field of Genetics in the United States. Your studies abroad will make you an expert in your field and the country will surely benefit from your expertise.

I would like to know your experience in the USA. So keep writing to me about life in America.

Wish you a happy time in the USA !

Yours sincerely

P.K. Sethi

D. Kannan
76 Temple Street
Montreal

September 16, ...

S. Balachandran
34/2 Kottayama Road
Frankfurl

Dear Balachandran

We were extremely happy to learn God has blessed you with a son. Please accept our heartiest congratulations.

Becoming a father is one of the milestones in the life of a person. It brings additional responsibilities and duties to a person. Write to me about your feelings on having a new member in your family. Now your wife's wish has also been fulfilled and I hope she no long suffers from bouts of depression. Please convey my congratulations to her also. My wife joins me sending her congratulations and good wishes to both of you.

How does your son look ? Does he resemble you ? We look forward to visiting you soon in order to meet Baby Balachandran.

With best regards,

Yours sincerely

D. Kannan

Robert Williams
Principal
Lawrence College
Blackpool

September 11, ...

Dr. and Mrs. M.L. Gera
Gera Chest Hospital
Safidon Road
London

Dear Dr. Gera,

Please accept my heartiest greetings on your 10th marriage anniversary which falls on 13th September.

The love and understanding which both you and Mrs. Gera have for each other is an example for all of us. I pray to God that this love between you goes on increasing as the time passes. May you have a long and blessed married life!

I wanted to visit you personally to convey my greetings. But some pressing engagements here have prevented me from doing so.

With love,

Yours truly

Robert Williams

Paresh Rawal
987 Dreamland Colony
Chandigarh

January 2, ...

R.S. Bhardwaj
89 Friends Colony
New Delhi

Dear Ramesh

Thanks for your new year card which I received this morning. I heartily reciprocate your good wishes and extend you my heartiest greetings for the new year. May this year bring love, prosperity and joy in your life!

With best wishes,

Yours truly

Paresh Rawal

XX. REQUESTS, ADVICES & SUGGESTIONS

186. Request for charitable contribution to a function

M.C. Cooper
Honey. Secretary
Servants of People Society
Moscow

Mr. Kasrpov
345 Briston Square
Moscow

Sir,

As you know the Servants of People Society of Moscow is a nonpolitical, non-profit society dedicated to the service of the poor, suffering and needy people of the society. You know there were unprecedented floods last year. Hundreds of people lost their lives and thousands were rendered without any means of livelihood. Our society is organising a cultural show in the Sports Stadium on 10th May, ... in aid of the Victims of the floods.

We approached Mr. David to compere the programe and also to present some interesting items. He has not only consented to grace the occasion but has also told that he would not charge anything for his services. A number of other prominent artistes of the city have also agreed to perform in the function free of charge. The proceeds of the programme will go to the aid of the flood victims.

We need at least ten thousand dollars for hiring the stadium and making other arrangements. You are a renowned philanthropist of the city. A number of charitable institutions are running on your generosity. You are requested kindly to donate this amount to our society so that we can make the function a success.

Thanking you in anticipation,

Yours faithfully

M.C. Cooper
Hony. Secretary

A. Thomson
CU/104 Friends Colony
New Delhi

October 10, ...

To

The General Manager
Mahangar Telephone Nigam Ltd
South Extension
New Delhi

Sir

I applied for a telephone connection three years ago but I have still not received the connection. As my needs are increasing, I wish to have a telephone connection immediately under "Own Your Telephone Instantly" scheme.

I am enclosing with this letter the requesite form duly filled in, with a bank draft No. 34797 dated October 10, drawn on the State Bank of India, for Rs. 30,000 towards the requisite fee under this scheme. If any more formalities are to be completed, please drop me a line and I'll do the needful.

You are requested to provide the telephone connection at an early date.

Thanking you,

Yours faithfully

(A. Thomson)

L. Dravid
Chartered Accountant
765, Suiss Appartments
Peking
December 12, ...

Mr. M. Leo
Director
Leor Sons
Caster Road
Hongkong

Sir

You know that I have been an apprentice chartered accountant with your firm for the last two years. I have learnt all the necessary matters concerning Chartered Accountancy and have satisfied you and others with my work.

Now an American based firm M/s Morgan Stanley Ltd. needs a chartered accountant for their firm. I am applying for this post. A recommendation letter from a firm of your stature would go a long way in my efforts to get the coveted job. Therefore, I request you kindly to issue me a letter of experience cum recommendation.

I hope, you will not turn down this request of mine.

Thanking you in advance,

Yours sincerely

L. Dravid

H. Kamath
Z-2 W.E.P.
New Delhi

June 02, ...

To

The Secretary
Community Centre
Diamond Apartments
New Delhi

Sir

The marriage of my daughter has been fixed for 25th of June. As there is no open space or a big hall near our residence, I would like to use the lawn in the centre of the Rajendra place Community centre for reception to the groom's party from 7.30 till about midnight on 25th June. I would also need the hall of the community of the same purpose.

I am sending with this application a cheque for Rs. 2500/- which is your usual fee for letting out the lawn and the hall for marriage functions or similar programmes.

I promise to leave the lawn and the hall in the neat and clean condition. I also undertake to bear the compensation for any damage etc. to the building and the lawn if it so occurs during the time I hire the lawn and the hall.

You are requested to intimate me your approval soon.

Thanking you,

Yours faithfully

H. Kamath

XXI. ADVICE AND SUGGESTIONS/ CONDOLENCE AND SYMPATHIES

---

190. *Advice to a son to avoid bad company*

B.K. Suharno
287 Sukarono Lane
Jakarta (Indonesia)

November 4, ...

Chunky Suharno
31 Boys Hostel
University of Indonesia
Jakarta

Dear Chunky

I have received a letter from your hostel warden as well as Principal that you have started mixing with bad boys and that has affected your studies adversely. He has also written that a number of times you have been punished on returning to your hostel late in the night in the company of such students who are considered good for nothing in the hostel.

It is needless to say that these reports have greatly shocked me. Dear Chunky, you are a promising young boy. You are highly talented and have always stood first in your class. But your bad company will surely spoil you. You are well aware of story of the rotten apple and the good ones and I needn't repeat it. As one rotten apple spoiled all good ones in the basket, in the same way one bad boy may spoil your life and put a brake on your academic as well as spiritual progress.

Therefore, I earnestly advice you to abstain from bad company. This is the time when you can make or mar your life. A few years of hard work will pave the way of lifelong comfort and joy. On the other hand if you make merry and neglect you studies for a few years now, you will repent for the whole life.

I hope you will act upon my advice and avoid had company.

Your father

B.K. Suharno

Madhuri Bijlani
676 Boulton Market
Karachi

January 18, ...

Pooja Shamin
872 Kadar Road
Karachi

Dear Pooja

I received your letter last week but could not reply to it at once a I was down with fever. You have asked me to advise you on a personal and confidential matter. It is so nice of you that you have confided in your aunt.

You have written in your letter that you love your boy friend Nadeem deeply and you want to marry each other soon. You have also written that your friendship in only one month old. In this connection, I want to say two things. The first is that you are still very young. You are only nineteen. Although legally it is your marriageable age, yet you are not mentally mature to shoulder the burden of a family.

Secondly, you are in B.Sc. final year. You should complete your studies before thinking of marriage. Marriage at this stage will hamper your studies also. A girl in these days should be able to stand on her own legs before marriage. So, it would be better for you to wait till you complete your studies and get a good job. If your boy friends has true love for you, he can wait for you this long.

In the mean time, you can go on meeting each other. This will have another advantage, You will be able to know and understand each other fully so that there would be no cause of regret later.

If there is any other thing you want my advice on, please be frank to write to me.

With love

Aunty Madhuri

S. Margret
Head, Dept. of English
M.D. University
Rajasthan

June 18, ...

Mr. V.S. Chhabra
Madhuban Cottage
23 Vrindaban Gardens
Gwalior (MP)

Dear Mr. Smith

Congratulations on your selection as a teacher at the prestigious Scindia Public School, Gwalior.

The job of a teacher carries a lot of responsibility. A teacher is the builder of nation. He moulds character of young students and makes them fit citizens. In the past India was famous all over the world for her great gurus and teachers. These teachers moulded the personality of their pupils and gave India her great philosophers, thinkers, scientists and statesmen. These teachers were themselves great. They practised what they preached. So their teaching had effect on their disciples.

As a teacher you will have be over board in your behaviour, conduct and personality. You should be a model before your students. It is a fact that the young students consciously or unconsciously follow their teachers. Whether you are teaching them are not you are influencing the thoughts and personalities of your students.

You should try to cultivate a method of teaching which is simple as well as effective. Your teaching should go straight to your students. Here I want to say a word about your own studies. A good teacher is always a student. He goes on learning new and new things all his life so that he can impart this knowledge to his students. So, let the whole knowledge be your province and never stop the process of learning.

Now, you have a lot of responsibility on your shoulders as a nation builder. I hope that you will act upon my advice and prove to be an excellent teacher.

Yours truly
S. Margret

Iftkhar Ali
375, Robinson Road
Singapore

August 13, ...

Dear Sushil

It was with a sense of disbelief and shock that I received the news of your mother's death. Her death is a loss to your whole family. It is a personal loss to me too. She was a kind and noble lady and treated me like her own son. She was a personification of fortitude and guided your family in a number of crises. Your father must be a shattered man to lose such a great life partner.

But human beings have no control over life and death. You have to bear the loss. Although the memory of such a lady can never be erased from mind, yet time will help you to get over the intensity of the shock. Please accept my heart—felt condolences. I pray to the God Almighty to grant peace to the departed soul and give you and your family strength to bear this loss.

Please write to me if I can do any thing for you in this hour of grief.

Yours sincerely

Iftkhar Ali

N. Crompton
346 Model Town
Auckland

July 8, ...

Rackson
643 Railway Road
Auckland

Dear Rackson

Your letter which I received yesterday conveyed to me the sad news that you have failed in the Medical College Entrance Examination. While it is really unpleasant news, it is not an occasion to feel heart broken.

I know that you prepared a lot kept awake till late nights preparing for this examination. However, success and failure are both parts of life. It is said that men learn more from failure than success. They teach us to take stock of ourselves and find out where we had missed in our efforts. They teach us to renew our efforts once again. You might have read the story of king Bruce who tried a number of times but failed. However, a humble spider taught him the lesson of relentless struggle till the gold is achieved. so failures are a blessing in disguise.

So, your failure in the medical Entrance test is hardly anything to feel heartbroken about. I know that you have the strength in you to achieve this goal. If you have failed once, I am sure you will come with flying colours the next time.

My good wishes are with you.

Yours truly

Crompton

Kalip Dumar
21 Flash Black Lane
Bollywood (India)

August 23, ...

Pooja Batra
45 Scandal Colony
Bollywood (India)

Dear Pooja

Yesterday I came across Kanil Apoor and he told me that you are a bit depressed because of having failed to win the award for best supporting actress for your role in 'Virasat'. I know that you gave a sterling performance in the film although it was your first film and you were confident of bagging the award for best supporting actress. Dear Pooja, the real thing in life is to have performed well. Awards and prizes are only secondary. The primary thing is the mental satisfaction.

The real reward of an actor or actress is the public acclaim. Your role in the film has been liked by all. The Press also wrote reviews about your performance. So you should not be put off by the decision of jury which is often influenced by personal choices also.

I wish you great success in your next film.

Yours sincerely

Kalip Dumar

XXII. CORRESPONDENCE BETWEEN A TENANT AND THE LANDLORD

196. To the tenant, enhancing rent

Somesh Bahuguna
274/5 Gandhi Nagar
Coimbatore
September 20, ...

Mr. Mahesh Chander
275/15 Nehru Nagar
Coimbatore

Dear Mr. Chander

You have been a tenant in my house for the last ten years. During this period we have maintained cordial relations. I thank you for maintaining the house as it were your own. You have acceded to all my requests regarding the proper upkeep of the house.

The house was let out to your for Rs. 1,900 per month. During this time, however, prices have increased many times. About four years ago, I wanted to enhance the rent but you said that you were facing economic difficulties and so I postponed the idea. But now I feel that a rent of Rs. 1,900/- per month for an independent house of 3 bed rooms is too meagre. I, therefore, enhance its rent to Rs. 2,800 per month. You will appreciate that even this enhanced rent is much lower than the prevailing rates.

I hope you will approve of this nominal enhancement in rent.

Thanking you,

Yours sincerely

Somesh Bahuguna

J.S. Shekhawat
78 Swami Mansingh Nagar
Bikaner

March 12, ...

Sh. Jaswant Sukhadia
453 MI Road
Bikaner

Dear Mr. Sukhadia

I have been living in your house for the last five years as a tenant. During these five years, the house has not been painted and repaired even once. The outer paint of the house has almost faded. On the inner walls of the room, the plast has peeled off at many places, giving the walls a shabby look. The ceiling of one room leaks badly and seepage has spread on the walls. As a result, ugly patches can be seen on the walls.

We are terribly embarrassed when our guests visit us and point out the shabby condition of the house. When I approached you last year for repairs, you showed your inability to do so on the ground financial stringency. If your budget does not allow you to carry out repairs, kindly allow me to do so myself. a sum of about 10,000/- is expected to be spent on carrying out painting and repairs. I will adjust this amount against the rent for the next four months. Thus it will not be a burden on you. Now I hope your budget will allow you.

Expecing an early reply and thanking you in advance,

Yours sincerely,

J.S. Shekhawat

Rafiq Ahmed
432 Tania Manzil
Abudabi

October 12, ...

Mr. Baslir Ahmed
54 Sikander Enclave
Abudabi

Dear Mr. Baslir

I am thankful to you for your help in making arrangements for the reception of groom's party at the time of my daughter's marriage last month. Now I wish to convey you another happy news. My son Ajay has got a job as an engineer at Ahmedabad. He joined his firm last week.

While we are happy at both these events, yet we face a peculiar difficulty now. As both my children have gone away, this house now proves too big for us. In fact when I go to my factory, my wife remains alone in the house and feels highly bored. There is no one to talk to her. Secondly, there is the matter of security also. when both of us have to remain out of the town, the house remains unguarded.

It is with this difficulty in view that I request you to allow us to sublet a portion of this house. One complete unit comprising two rooms, a kitchen and a bathroom can be sublet. I wish to sublet this portion to a close friend of mine. He is thorough gentleman and I take full responsibility about his behaviour. Of course, this would not mean any disadvantage to you in rent. I will collect the rent proportionate to the portion sublet to him and you'll continue receiving the rent which I have already been paying you.

I hope you will agree to this arrangement.

Thanking you,

Yours sincerely

Rafiq Ahmed

Registered

Manoj Bhandari
23 Octavio Street
Meerut

January 24, ...

Mr. S. Paul
B-75 Tilak Nagar
Meerut

Dear Mr. Paul

When I let out the house to you two years ago, it was with a mutual verbal contract that you will not use the house for any purpose other than that of residence.

But my consternation, I have found that you have started operating a small flour mill after installing machinery in two of the rooms. On my visit to the house I found that the constant rumbling of the machinery was affecting the strength of walls. Already the cement plaster has started showing signs of cracks. Moreover, other residents around the house have complained to me of the constant disturbance to them because of the continuous sound of grinding stone mills. This is a serious matter of breach of trust.

Therefore, through this letter, I give you a notice of three months from hence to vacate the house. If you fail to do within this period, I will be compelled to file a law suit against you to get the house vacated.

Thanking you,

Yours sincerely

Manoj Bhandari

Dave Daniel
45 Main Road
Taipai

July 8, ...

Mr. Scott B.
23/6 Chuia Road
Taipai

Dear Mr. Scott

This is my second letter reminding you to pay your outstanding rent payment for the last ten months. I have been very lenient with you during this period and have made a number of verbal requests to you. Even my letter asking you to pay the rent was a gentle reminder. But I find that all these requests have fallen on deaf ears.

Now, through this letter, I give you a final notice that you must clear the outstanding rent within twenty days of the receipt of this letter. You may make the payment through a crossed cheque or demand draft for $ 10,000, which amounts to rent for ten months. If you fail to clear the outstanding rent payment, I shall be forced to file a law suit against you and ask the court to get the house vacated.

Thanking you,

Sincerely yours

Dave Daniel

NOTES